SPIRITS
OF THE
JAGUAR

SPIRITS
OF THE
JAGUAR

THE NATURAL HISTORY AND
ANCIENT CIVILIZATIONS OF THE
CARIBBEAN AND CENTRAL AMERICA

PAUL REDDISH

BBC BOOKS

ACKNOWLEDGEMENTS

This is, traditionally, the place to thank all concerned in the making of this book; and this will be duly and gratefully done in the following paragraphs. But first I wish to express my gratitude to all my friends, family and colleagues who have put up with my 'temporary madness' during the writing of the book. Their humour and patience with an 'over-excited child' dashing headlong from filming to writing to editing and back to filming has been my salvation. These unnamed saints know who they are; and to them goes my greatest thanks. Sanity may, or may not, return.

This book has been written to accompany the television series of the same name. I have been very lucky to have a talented and generous team. Mark Jacobs, Sarah Byatt, Neil Lucas, Mark Flowers, Phil Savoie, Andrew Murray have all worked to realize our dream of combining natural and cultural history. They have been supported by Sue Storey, Fiona Marsh, Lynn Sinclair and Julia McDade. Television is above all team work and to them all I express my gratitude.

This has been my first 'bash' at a book and I have been helped by the talents of many people at BBC Books. Sheila Ableman was brave enough to ask me to write; Martha Caute, Frances Abraham and Barbara Nash stoic enough to put up with the rollercoaster ride to publication. This book is a product of all our efforts.

Books emerge slowly from snippets of stories, forgotten fragments of information. In the slow process of shaping these, it is easy to overlook the originator. I would like to acknowledge all the scientists whose work I have mentioned here. It is their original research that has uncovered the remarkable story of Central America and the Caribbean. *Paul Reddish*

This book accompanies the television series *Spirits of the Jaguar*, first broadcast in 1996.
The series was produced by the Natural History Unit, BBC Bristol
Series Producer: Paul Reddish   Producer: Mark Jacobs

Published by BBC Books, a division of BBC Worldwide Limited,
Woodlands, 80 Wood Lane, London W12 0TT
First published 1996   © Paul Reddish 1996
The moral rights of the author have been asserted
ISBN 0 563 38743 2

Designed by DW Design London
Picture research by Frances Abraham   Maps by Line & Line
Printed and bound in Great Britain by Butler & Tanner Ltd., Frome and London
Colour separations by Radstock Reproductions, Midsomer Norton
Jacket printed by Lawrence Allen Ltd., Weston-super-Mare

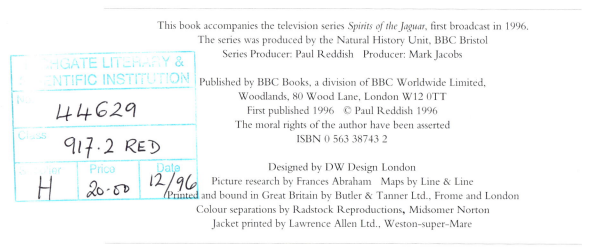
FRONTISPIECE: A male quetzal at the nest-hole reveals the full glory of its feathers.

CONTENTS

INTRODUCTION

The Land of Dazzling Wildlife and Lost Civilizations

Central America and the Caribbean are wondrous. Biologically, they can claim to be the richest place on earth, and the region is also home to the greatest civilizations of the New World: the Maya and the Aztecs. This book follows a fascinating journey through time: connecting drifting continents to flying frogs; violent volcanic eruptions to the movement of monkeys; and blood sacrifices and astronomy to uncertain seasons. Starting with a blank expanse of ocean, the book looks at the making of the land, and the arrival of the plants and animals. Jaguars and hummingbirds, quetzals and crocodiles, parrots and iguanas all have a part in the epic story of the making of the region.

Any story about Central America and the Caribbean that left out people would be incomplete. Humans have had a huge impact on the land. This book examines not just the influence of people on the wildlife, but also the power of the place on the minds of the native people. Wet and dry seasons, hurricanes and volcanic eruptions, and animals, such as the resplendent quetzal and jaguar, have all influenced the development of the great civilizations of the Maya and Aztecs. The growth of native cultures from their natural world is the subject of the middle part of the book.

The arrival of Europeans transformed the Caribbean and Central America. Novel ideas, new domesticated plants and animals, and a more advanced technology, changed the local wildlife and cultures. Today the process continues, but conservation is now a part of the many influences on this most fascinating part of the world. This is an epic tale, spanning 150 million years, of 'the spirits of the jaguar'.

The two geographical areas of Central America and the Caribbean are intimately linked. They form part of one of the earth's great crustal plates. Their intertwined histories have dictated the plants and animals to be found in the region.

The first part of the book tells how Central America came to be the link, the 'land bridge', between two great continents. The making of the land bridge created new opportunities for wildlife. An incredible diversity of plants and animals sprang from the earth-moving events that created the land bridge.

The meandering strip of land that tenuously connects the two great continents is one of the most marvellous places on earth. Costa Rica, only half the size of the state of Tennessee, has 850 species of birds, more than the whole of North America. There is an amazing array of frogs, and more bees, wasps and bats than the whole northern continent. This is a paradise, but a bewildering one.

The forests hide such colour beneath their dark green canopies. Jewel-like

PREVIOUS PAGES: The Virgin Isles, playground and paradise, but little is known about the true nature of the Caribbean.

birds, such as manakins and tanagers, conceal their splendours in the deepest shade. There are still insects, unknown to us, awaiting the patient scientist. There are birds whose nests have never been found. The night air is filled with the strange calls of frogs and insects, bats sweep the humid air, and poisonous snakes lie coiled in wait. This is the mystery and majesty of the tropics; there is so much to take in, so much still to understand. The forests are overpowering at a first glance. Bathed by sunlight and rain, life has run riot. There is seeming chaos: leaves, lianas, vines and tree trunks of all sizes, create a three-dimensional maze of mind-numbing complexity; unseen birds call, their alien cries adding to the sense of wonder. Is there any way to understand this wondrous, attractive, daunting world?

The area of Central America is small in comparison to its neighbours, the continents of North and South America, but it links them, and much of their wildlife mingles on its fertile volcanic soils. The biological richness of the region comes from the meeting of creatures from the north and south. The land bridge is a novel feature on the face of the earth. It wasn't there a few million years ago.

The area covered in this book extends beyond the isthmus, the classic land bridge of Panama, Costa Rica and Nicaragua, to include the wonderful country of Mexico.

Mexico is the third most biologically-rich country on the planet, but that is not the immediate perception – spicy Mexican food, Mariachi bands and the terrible pollution of its capital Mexico City, are more likely to spring to mind than the spectacular scenery and wilderness. Yet, fringing the Valley of Mexico, there are snow-capped volcanoes with their own wonderful endemic creatures. Beyond the volcanoes lie pine and oak woodlands, deserts, strange spiny forests, lush rainforests, sweltering tropical swamps and mangrove-fringed coral reefs. It is this diversity of habitat that explains the richness of species of Mexico. Pumas prowl through steep-sloped woods, while, lower down the same mountains, jaguars strike dread in the hearts of man and animal alike. Golden eagles soar over windswept, craggy, volcanic peaks and, several thousand feet below, toucans and parrots fly, the glittering gems of the rainforest.

The great storehouse of species of Central America played a large part in the populating of the Caribbean. The story of how plants and animals arrived on the remote islands is a tale that cannot be told without understanding the birth process of the Caribbean. The real Caribbean is as little known as the true nature of Mexico. Behind the glossy façade of the holiday brochure lies an archipelago of curious and unique animals.

There are over 10 000 species of flowering plants on the islands of the Caribbean, and a third of these are found nowhere else on earth. Over three-

quarters of the 350 or so species of Caribbean butterflies are found only on the islands. Many are confined to just one island.

There are 451 species of reptiles in the West Indies. A decent number, you might think, but pathetic really compared with the riches of Central America. What is remarkable is that 93 per cent of these reptiles are unique to the Caribbean. The story is similar for frogs. Ninety-eight per cent of the 174 kinds of Antillean amphibians are found nowhere else on earth.

The West Indies has an extraordinary number of unique birds. Only Hawaii and the Galapagos have a higher percentage of endemic birds, and they are far more remote than any Caribbean island. There are 210 species of land birds and 151 of these are unique.

The reasons for such high numbers of unique animals is one of the great mysteries that has taxed scientists for over a hundred years. How did these animals get to the islands? Why are they different from their nearest relatives? Why is there such a poor diversity of animals in comparison to mainland regions? The answer lies in the history of the islands. This book tells the story of how the Caribbean islands were born in the vastness of the Pacific and then travelled to their present positions. The islands' journey had a profound effect on how animals and plants reached their tropical shores.

The islands are not uniform: they can be placed in groups that reflect their physical and biological history. A quick geography lesson is necessary if the reader is to fully appreciate the ripping yarns of violent volcanoes, moving islands and rafting reptiles.

The land area of the West Indies is 240 000 square kilometres, similar to that of the United Kingdom, but parcelled into numerous small and large islands. In fact, there are so many scattered islands that it is a very confusing part of the world. So what are we talking about when using the terms West Indies, Caribbean Islands, and the more arcane names: the Lesser and Greater Antilles?

The term West Indies only adds to the confusion, for it is a hangover from Columbus and his stubborn belief that he had sailed to the Indies, the spice islands, and Japan. The names of most of the Greater Antilles are Spanish, reflecting the long colonial period. After all, this was the birthplace of the European 'adventure' in the New World. The West Indies can be divided into three sub-regions. From north to south these are: the Bahamian archipelago along with the Turks and Caicos islands; the larger islands of the Greater Antilles; and the smaller isles of the Lesser Antilles.

The scarlet macaw is one of the most spectacular of Mexico's pantheon of birds.

This book examines each of these three biological sub-regions of the West Indies. The Greater Antilles are the biggest islands and the most richly populated by plants and animals. They share a common geological history, which helps explain their biological nature. They are the subjects of the next three chapters.

The Lesser Antilles, which form the easterly edge of the Caribbean, are much more sparsely populated. This is due to the nature of their fiery origins, quite separate from their larger cousins to the north. Their story is the subject of chapter five.

The Bahamian archipelago to the north of the line of the Greater Antilles are outside the Caribbean proper, yet their biological and social history has been connected to the islands to the south. They are, broadly speaking, the northern outposts of the Caribbean islands.

The story of how people arrived in the region is different from that of the plants and other animals. The first humans on the continent were hunters who crossed over from Siberia by a dry-land connection now submerged under the Bering Sea. The story of the transformation of nomadic mammoth-hunters into sedentary farmers is a fascinating one. The domestication of maize happened in Mexico and it revolutionized peoples' lives and led to the first great civilization of Central America: the Olmecs.

The Maya civilization grew from the forests of southern Mexico, Guatemala and Honduras. The climate, plants and animals, helped shape the Maya mind and influenced the course of the burgeoning culture. The civilization collapsed suddenly and mysteriously about a thousand years ago.

Long before that, the ancestors of the Taino set sail from South America. These bold explorers in their dug-out canoes were destined to be the people of the Caribbean. Their culture, mythology and religion were shaped by the nature of their new island homes. The Taino have the dubious honour to be the people who welcomed Columbus to the 'New World'. They were a gentle spiritual people with few of the material trappings of civilization.

In complete contrast are the Aztecs. They came from the northern 'wastelands' of Mexico; the deserts and thorn scrubs. Their world view was coloured by the harsh unpredictable landscape, and the seemingly endless enemies they had to face. The Aztecs built a great empire on military might. Yet one of the prime purposes of this empire was to provide human sacrificial victims to assuage their fierce gods. The Aztecs had a cataclysmic world view.

The arrival of Columbus on the shores of the Caribbean was to change the whole world. The local impact was devastating. The Taino were decimated. Within forty years, the Aztec empire had been toppled by Cortés and his conquistadors. The mixing of the old and new world had a profound influence on the wildlife and people of Central America.

Much of the history of the region for the last 200 years is depressing. The Caribbean has suffered more than its share of environmental degradation. Central America has been logged and planted. But the people and the place are resilient, and new conservation efforts on the islands and the mainland leave room for hope.

After this introductory chapter, the book follows a broadly historical line. The first part considers how Central America and the Caribbean were born and grew into their present shapes. This intriguing process has had a major impact on the plants and animals of the region. The who's-who and who's-where has been dictated by the shifting islands.

The second part of the book covers the story of people. Starting with the arrival of the first hunters in Central America, it looks at how the place, its geography, climate, plants and animals, have influenced the growth of civilizations. There are separate chapters on the Maya, the Taino and the Aztecs. The last two chapters consider the meeting of east and west, and the history of the region since Columbus.

CENTRAL AMERICA AND THE CARIBBEAN

UNITED STATES OF AMERICA

Rio Grande

CHICHIMEC

Gulf of Mexico

M E X I C O

Pánuco

TOLTEC

Tula •

Mexico City •

AZTEC

Balsas

OLMEC

Oaxaca •

ZAPOTEC

Piedras Negras •

YUCATÁN

MAYA

Hondo

BELIZE

Uaxactún •

Motagua

HONDURAS

P a c i f i c   O c e a n

GUATEMALA

San •
Salvador

EL SALVADOR

COSTA RICA

Map showing Pre-Columbian Settlements page 106
Map showing Maya Settlements page 126
Map showing the Aztec World page 170

0   Kilometres   500

0   Miles   500

FLORIDA

Atlantic Ocean

GREAT ABACO ISLAND

The Bahamas

SAN SALVADOR

CAICOS ISLANDS

La Isabela (old town and sugar plantation)

VIRGIN ISLANDS

TURKS ISLAND

Windward Islands

Zapata swamp

INAGUA ISLAND

Hispaniola

Samana Bay

Luquillo Mountains

CUBA

Navidad (destroyed fort)

● **Ponce**

GUADELOUPE

ISLA DE JUVENTUD

Greater Antilles

HAITI

Santo Domingo

PUERTO RICO

DOMINICA

Lake Enriquillo

MARTINIQUE

GRAND CAYMAN

DOMINICAN REPUBLIC

ST LUCIA

CAYMAN IS

Lesser Antilles

BARBADOS

Blue Mountains

ST VINCENT

JAMAICA

GRENADA

Caribbean Sea

TOBAGO

TRINIDAD

Orinoco Delta

NICARAGUA

Orinoco

Santo Domingo

Panama Canal

VENEZUELA

PANAMA

COLOMBIA

BRAZIL

Part 1

THE NATURE
OF THE
CARIBBEAN
AND
CENTRAL AMERICA

Chapter 1

The Great Mystery

Perhaps there is no greater puzzle in biogeography than that of how creatures arrive on islands; and the Caribbean, full of islands, is full of intrigue. The insular nature of the tiny todies (see page 22), is hard to explain, but there are tougher conundrums. How did millipedes reach Cuba? There are many kinds of millipedes on the island, yet they can't fly, aren't known to swim well, dislike salt water and, despite their numerous legs, no one would claim they walked there. Why are there so few mammals on the islands? How did tiny frogs, no bigger than a thumbnail, come to dominate the night sounds on most of the islands? And there are many other, equally improbable, islanders whose means of arrival demands an explanation.

The enigma is all the more curious when you look at the who's-who of Caribbean life. In general, plants and animals on the islands are similar but different from those found on the surrounding mainland. Not only are individual species different from their continental cousins, but the mix of animals and plants is different. There are flightless insects, snakes, tiny birds, such as hummingbirds, and small freshwater fish, but no jaguars or deer, no large birds, such as toucans or turkeys. Overall, the diversity of life is much less out on the islands. Why is the roll-call of Caribbean island life so different from that of the mainland where it is assumed the ancestral forms came from?

How did the plants and animals get there?

In the last century and the early part of this one there were two competing schools of thought on how animals came to be on the Caribbean islands. They were examples of two more general theories on the distributions of living things. The first proposal was that the plants and animals had drifted or rafted over from North or South America – involuntary sailors swept to their new island homes by sea currents and ocean breezes. The second idea was that there were 'land bridges' that once connected the islands with the mainland. This, too, solved the problem of how the ancestors, the founding 'Adam and Eve', had managed to reach the island. The sea level had then risen, or the land sunk beneath the waves, to cover the creatures' tracks.

The 'land bridge' concept was conceived to explain a greater, more general problem: curious 'anomalies' that were being discovered in the distribution of animals on the major continents. There is a group of flightless birds (the ratites), which has members on all the southern land masses: ostriches in Africa, rheas in

PREVIOUS PAGES: The green turtle, a great ocean wanderer,
and a creature whose long history matches that of the region.

South America, and emus in Australia. They could not have winged it between the continents. There are primitive freshwater lungfish on the same continents – they could not have swum the thousands of kilometres across the oceans. In fact, they could not have finned a furlong in the sea because the high salt concentration would have killed them. There were fossil finds of a giant dinosaur, titanosaurus, in South America, Africa and India. Again no one was proposing that this behemoth doggy-paddled across the oceans. By connecting the continents by narrow strips of land, however, none of the dinosaurs would have needed to get its feet wet, the lungfish could have stayed in sweet water, and the ancestral ostrich would have been able to strut between continents. A good theory, then, but there were problems.

A map of the world, drawn by an early land-bridge proponent would look absurd to our eyes. But to explain all the distributions, a network of attenuated strips of land had to reach from continent to continent. The land bridges not only stretched across the globe, they also stretched credulity to breaking point. If all the islands were linked by ephemeral earthy umbilicals, what colossal complexity. Charles Darwin commented that palaeontologists seem to 'build land bridges (or isthmian links) as easy as a chef makes pancakes'.

In the Caribbean context there were more problems with land bridges than their clumsy gigantic size. As biologists discovered each new species on the islands, and linked it to a putative ancestor in North, Central or South America, then an explanation was required. A land bridge was evoked for every case, leaving the geologists to find an impossible number of fluctuations of sea level. One problem had simply been traded for another bigger one: what could explain the oceans' oscillations? The sea level needed to move up and down like a yo-yo. This difficulty was added to, when oceanographers came to measure the depths of the ocean. Many of the proposed submerged land bridges simply were not there.

There was also a problem in the logic of the land bridge. It was put forward to explain the existence of a plant or animal on an island, but a corridor of land between island and mainland would allow not just the species in question, but a whole gamut of other organisms, to cross. And, for that matter, it would allow islanders to cross back to the mainland. So islands would end up having the same plants and animals as the continents and lots of them, but this is patently not so. Ironically, it was the unique island creatures and the lack of diversity that demanded an explanation in the first place. Land bridges were too indiscriminate and were two-way streets. What was needed was a more difficult route that favoured some species; and a route that was more directional.

Before leaving the land-bridge concept, it is worth mentioning that, while it fares badly in trying to explain the colonization of the large Caribbean

ABOVE: The greatest mountain range on earth? The mid-Atlantic ridge runs the length of the ocean.
Its discovery gave credence to the theory of plate tectonics.

OPPOSITE: The tody, a flamboyant bundle of feathers. The presence of these tiny birds (9 cm)
on the remote islands demands an explanation.

islands, it is still the best model for two other important events in the story of the Central American region. The next part of this book examines the great interchange of animals between North and South America, along 'The Land Bridge' that today is Panama. And the colonization of Trinidad and Tobago, told in chapter 5, is a classic example of a land bridge created and destroyed by changing sea levels. But back to the conundrum of Cuba and the other large Caribbean islands: how *did* the plants and animals get there?

What of the other idea, that animals rafted across? Does it fare any better? It does in the sense that it neatly and discretely ferries the founding fathers and mothers to the islands. They alone are on the raft. It is also a one-way process, another major plus. But there are problems. Like the land-bridge idea, it stretches the boundaries of belief a bit. It is a process that has not been tested or observed in any rigorous manner. The poor marooned creatures are supposed to have stayed alive at sea on a loose raft of logs or a tangle of twigs and branches. How long did they stay at sea, and why didn't they starve, or die of thirst, drown, or be killed by the waves of salt water that surely must have washed over the crude craft? What were the odds of the raft and its sorry living cargo drifting on for years in the open sea rather than brushing up against a beach? Would there have been any food for them on their new island home? And even if all these conditions were met, would they have felt like propagating the species after such a gruelling sea voyage? In short, rafting to an island is an improbable event. But perhaps a time-scale of hundreds of thousands, if not millions of years, was great enough to make up for the rarity of successful rafting? For a period, these two opposing theories – land bridge and rafting – were all that was available to explain one of the great biological mysteries.

The plate-tectonics revolution

If you can't bring millipedes to Cuba, then Cuba must go to the millipedes. This, in a sense, is what a revolutionary idea suggested. Instead of explaining how plants and animals moved on to static land masses, the theory of *continental drift* moved the land to the animals. Bizarre, non-intuitive, yes, but it all started from a simple observation last century and became an insight that millions of schoolchildren have shared ever since.

In 1858 Antonio Snider, an American living in Paris, published a map that showed the continents of Africa and South America fitted snugly together. His insight was to note the obvious parallels of the coastlines of the two continents. Surely this must be more than coincidence? Many a primary schoolchild, versed in the art of jigsaws, has seen the same pattern on the classroom globe, and, unconstrained by the adult baggage of theory, mentally connected the continents.

The problem, however, was how could vast continents move? Snider called on God. The original 'super-continent' had been rent by the biblical deluge to create Africa and South America, with the South Atlantic in between. The problem of what force could have propelled the continents beset the German meteorologist, Alfred Wegener, who proposed the most powerful case for continental drift in 1912. Wegener managed to complete the jigsaw and connect all the continents into one giant land mass which he called Pangaa (now known as Pangea).

While the moving of lands helped to explain the otherwise perplexing distribution of many living and fossilized creatures, without a mechanism to drive the continents the idea appeared as far-fetched as the tenuous 'land bridges'. In fact more so, for, in Wegener's theory, whole continents had to somehow slide over the ocean floor. Even Wegener admitted defeat as to how solid rock might glide over equally solid ocean basement. The result was stalemate for over thirty years, with scientists split over whether continents moved or not. Some called the idea 'a beautiful dream'. In the 1920s, the former president of the American Philosophical Society warmed to the subject when he described the theory of continental drift as 'utter dammed rot'.

A mechanism was needed. The first clues were to come from the dark depths of the ocean. After the Second World War the sea floor was surveyed by the new advanced technology of echo-sounding. In particular, the Atlantic Ocean was comprehensively scanned. The results were surprising. The sea floor was not a monotonous abyssal plain – there were mountains down there. In fact, there was a whole mountain range that stretched north to south down the centre of the ocean (see page 23).

To add to the intrigue, the mountain chain was symmetrical and had a great valley along its spine. What did it all mean? Some geologists suggested that the sea floor was spreading out equally in both directions from the mid-oceanic ridge. Earthquake activity hinted at the dynamic nature of the submarine mountain range. If fresh molten rock, magma, was welling up and pushing out equally, then this sea-floor spreading could be the motor that was moving the continents. The truth is that the nature of the forces that move the giant plates is still not fully understood. But the fact that the sea floor was spreading, as new sea floor was manufactured in mid ocean, was confirmed in the 1960s by looking at the magnetic orientation of the rocks either side of the ridge.

The rocks of the sea floor are mainly basalts, which contain a large amount of iron in the form of magnetite crystals. The direction of magnetization of the crystals depends on the earth's own magnetic field. It should be constant, then. But when the sea floor was surveyed with airborne magnetometers, a very curious result was obtained. The sea floor was composed of a patchwork of rock

of opposite magnetic orientations. The position of the magnetized rocks was not random: they lay in a series of parallel bands that ran north to south.

The poles may seem permanent, but, in fact, they have reversed many times over the millions of years of earth's long history. The South Pole has become the North and vice versa. Don't ask why – that's another mystery to be solved! But the changing polarity of the earth did help explain the parallel bands of magnetism of the sea floor. At the instant of the upwelling, the liquid lava cooled and the direction of the magnetism in the iron-bearing minerals was frozen at the same orientation as that of the poles at that moment. The parallel lines of magnetization, which were symmetrical about the mid-oceanic ridge, were like a tape-recording of the drama of the sea floor's widening: each new episode happening with the poles switched either north or south. The continents were moving *along with* the ocean floors, not *over* them as Wegener had suggested. Even as you read this book, the process continues: the Atlantic is growing and, each year, Europe and Africa are a few centimetres further from the Americas.

The problem of how the continents might move seemed resolved but, as is ever the case, one person's solution is another's problem. What happened to all the new 'extra' sea floor that was being produced mid ocean? Surely the ocean basement had to be consumed at the same rate; if it wasn't, the earth must surely be expanding like a balloon. As this is not a serious suggestion, then a destructive mechanism was needed to match the creative processes of the mid-ocean ridges. The answer was that the oldest sea floor – that is, the edge of the plate furthest from the spreading centre – was disappearing under the neighbouring plate, back into the melting pot. Recycling has a long history on earth! The oceanic plates were operating like conveyor belts, moving the continents upon their backs, with new ocean floor being generated at one edge and old rocks disappearing at the other.

Plate tectonics, as this came to be known, is the theory of the movements of the huge crustal 'plates' of the planet. There is still work to be done on the mechanism of plate motions, but the theory has helped to explain many of the paradoxical distributions of animals and plants. It plays a major role in the story of the Caribbean and the distribution of its inhabitants.

The birth of the Caribbean

Eerie lights flicker deep in the ocean, a crimson red glow floods the inky night waters, stutters and is extinguished. The hiss of steam, the fierce bubbling and spitting of super-heated waters, and an explosion rents the air. A lone isle of

---

Island-making in progress. Hawaii today may give us a picture of the Caribbean isles 100 million years ago.

smouldering cinders pokes out above the waves of the mighty ocean. Pounded by the sea, the island disappears only to explode back above the surface. These violent events herald the birth of the Caribbean islands. Yet the location is far out in the Pacific, a thousand kilometres from the coast of South America. Sounds strange, and it is, for only since the plate-tectonics revolution have such scenarios made any sense. The story that follows is still being worked out, and will surely change as more information becomes available. But, for now, the story goes something like this.

The time must have been around 150 to 130 million years ago. The exact date may never be known, but the process of island-making had been going on for millions of years. The oldest rocks of the Pacific sea floor had been disappearing under the western edge of the newly forming Caribbean. As the rocks dipped down they melted, to 'bubble' back up as magma, which eventually reached the surface of the sea floor. It took many more submarine volcanic explosions and outpourings before a lone island was born. It was the first of many summits of submarine volcanoes that appeared along the line of the 'subducting' Pacific plate. This was the violent beginning of the Caribbean islands, as a chain of fresh volcanic isles.

Were there any witnesses to this extraordinary birth? It would seem impossible that we should ever know, for the explosions happened so long ago. Yet a fossil discovered in Cuba suggests that there might have been an observer. Limestones laid down in shallow tropical seas have given up the remains of a pterosaur. There were many of these ancient flying reptiles in their heyday. Some were great gliders that drifted over the oceans, and probably lived by scooping fish from the surface waters. One of these magnificent creatures may have seen the islands before falling to its death in the shallow fringing seas, to be entombed and fossilized.

By 120 million years ago, the proto-Caribbean isles had grown to look like the current Aleutian Island chain. They stretched 2000 kilometres, from off the west coast of Mexico to the coast of Ecuador in South America. Beneath the islands, plumes of hot magma or molten rock rose towards the surface from the zone of melting, 30 to 100 kilometres below. Over the crowns of these giant blobs of lighter molten rock, tens of kilometres across, volcanoes formed like pimples. But what pimples! Steep-sided island volcanoes are the most violent of nature's fireworks. At night the line of islands must have glowed red as lava oozed, exploded, and poured from the earth. The sky would have filled frequently with dust and ash as explosions rent the air. Volcanic activity would have continued to raise new islands out of the sea. In addition, individual cones, as they grew larger, would have merged to form long thin islands oriented along the line of the island arc.

There is no available evidence about the inhabitants from this early period in the history of the Caribbean islands. The black lava beaches were most likely empty of any life, with one possible exception. Marine turtles are a very ancient group of animals whose behaviour has changed little over the millennia, for the very good reason that they are so successful. To reproduce, the females need deserted beaches where their eggs will not be stolen by hungry predators. Islands are ideal, as they often have fewer predators than the mainland. Back 120 million years ago, the burgeoning Caribbean isles must have offered ideal nesting grounds to green turtles. The thought of turtles hauling themselves out of the ancient tropical Pacific Ocean, under a glowering volcanic sky, and sculling across a black sand beach to produce the next generation is most seductive, but it is only speculation.

For 50 million years the proto-Caribbean islands remained strictly Pacific, but this curious state of affairs was about to come to an end. The islands were starting out on a great voyage!

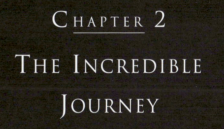

CHAPTER 2

THE INCREDIBLE

JOURNEY

A round 100 million years ago a great change took place. Under a perpetual pall of smoke the islands were still growing. Fierce volcanic activity spewed forth a concoction of rocks, cinders and dust. The line of the islands still lay in a north-south orientation stretching from present-day Mexico towards western Colombia. The dramatic event was the reversal of the direction of subduction. It sounds nothing special, but when the sea floor of the Proto-Caribbean began to sink under the islands, instead of the ancient Pacific, then the islands were free to move.

The mid-Atlantic spreading centre continued its activity and the Atlantic Ocean grew ever wider. North and South America were both travelling rapidly west (a scorching ten centimetres a year), consuming the descending Pacific-floor plate. The line of islands, now gobbling up ocean floor to the east of it, moved towards the two continents. Tectonically speaking, the Proto-Caribbean Islands, born in the Pacific, were now setting sail. The chain of islands was on the move, heading eastward towards the gap between North and South America

The docking period

The northern portion of the chain of islands must have collided with the Yucatán region of Mexico around 80 million years ago. The rest of the island arc continued to move east, riding over and consuming the proto-Caribbean sea floor. There was a general uplifting and deforming of the islands as they were squeezed into the gap between Yucatán and Colombia. There could have been a continuous land connection between North and South America for periods at this time as the islands slipped through the bottleneck. More likely were short-lasting intermittent connections along the chain of islands, as they were constantly remodelled by the forces of vulcanism and tectonics. The crumpling, ripping and deforming, as the islands squeezed past South America, left them in a great curving arc, with the northern portion, which was now brushing against Mexico, facing due east-west, while the southern end was oriented due north from the north-west corner of Colombia.

For the next 20 million years the northern section, those bits that were destined to become the Greater Antilles, remained close to, and often connected to, the North American continent. There was an opportunity for these mobile islands to take passengers on board. Here was a case of the islands coming to the creatures not the other way round. But did any creature take the chance to slip on board?

PREVIOUS PAGES: The eggs of an *Eleutherodactylus* frog, one of the first passengers on the mobile islands. The egg completes its development to adult frog within its miniature transparent sphere.

The first stowaways

Eleutherodactylus is the difficult-to-pronounce name of a gigantic genus of frogs. (A genus is the level of taxonomic grouping above individual species.) The frogs are small, in fact so small that many are nowhere near as long as the name they go under. The smallest found to date is from eastern Cuba, and at 0.9 centimetres it is the smallest four-legged creature in the world. That claim to fame, and the fact that the genus contains over 500 species, which makes it the largest in the vertebrate animal kingdom, are as much as you can say about *Eleutherodactylus* frogs. Except, that is, for one important biological fact.

Eleutherodactylus frogs all have direct development of their young - the tadpole stage takes place inside the egg. These frogs have freed themselves from the need for water in which to breed. The tadpoles' water is the fluid inside the large egg. They hatch out having already metamorphosed into a diminutive version of their small parents. This liberation from streams and lakes may help to explain the success of these frogs. They have been exceptional pioneers, able to colonize great swathes of the Americas, unfettered by nearness of water. Other than that, they are small, undistinguished and olive brown. But they may be the best evidence of stowaways on the mobile islands. There are two regions which are particularly blessed with species of these frogs: northern South America and the Caribbean islands.

Professor Blair Hedges of Pennsylvania State University has been studying the genetics of these frogs, to try to discover their relationships. The technique Professor Hedges uses is to compare cell proteins, such as serum albumin. These proteins are subject to the forces of evolution just as the whole animal is. Over time, the proteins mutate to form new molecules. The speed at which this happens is thought to be relatively constant; a sort of background random variation, as the generations roll by. Specific locations along the chain of amino acids that make up the protein are compared to give a measure of how related, or unrelated, two animals are. More than that, a whole group of animals, such as the *Eleutherodactylus* frogs, can be studied so that a phylogenetic tree, or line of relatedness, can be elucidated. This 'family tree' is a picture of the likely evolutionary history of the group. So, by studying proteins, and looking at the current distributions of the frogs, Professor Hedges can gain glimpses of where the frogs evolved and how and where they then moved.

There is another exciting element to this work. As the speed of change of the amino acids that compose proteins is relatively constant, so the amount of change is a measure of time. This is a molecular clock, with a 'second hand' that counts in millions of years. Protein analysis can give us not only a measure of evolution but a time-scale. This is a new technique which complements the study of similarities

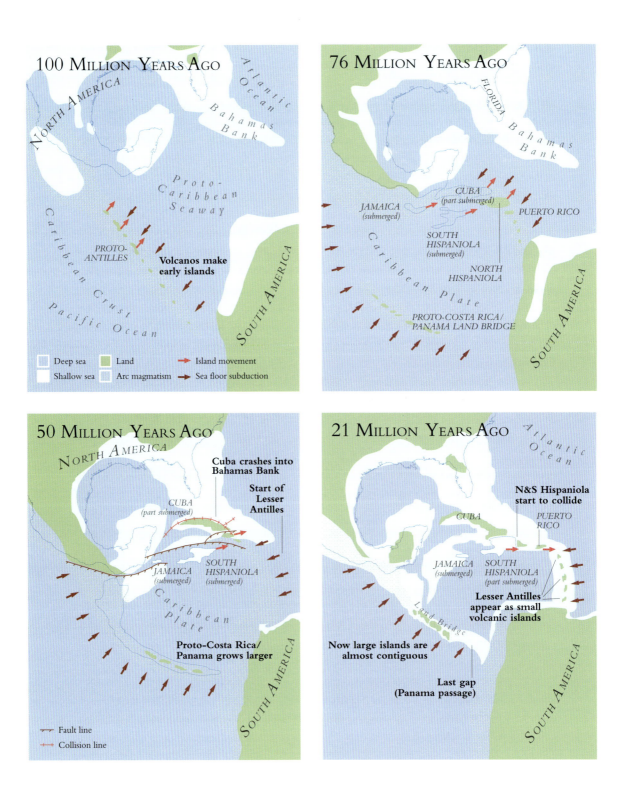

100 Million Years Ago

NORTH AMERICA

Atlantic Ocean

Bahamas Bank

Proto-Caribbean Seaway

Caribbean Crust

PROTO-ANTILLES

Volcanos make early islands

Pacific Ocean

SOUTH AMERICA

Deep sea   Land   → Island movement

Shallow sea   Arc magmatism   → Sea floor subduction

76 Million Years Ago

FLORIDA

Bahamas Bank

CUBA (part submerged)

JAMAICA (submerged)

PUERTO RICO

SOUTH HISPANIOLA (submerged)

NORTH HISPANIOLA

Caribbean Plate

PROTO-COSTA RICA/ PANAMA LAND BRIDGE

SOUTH AMERICA

50 Million Years Ago

NORTH AMERICA

Cuba crashes into Bahamas Bank

Start of Lesser Antilles

CUBA (part submerged)

JAMAICA (submerged)

SOUTH HISPANIOLA (submerged)

Caribbean Plate

Proto-Costa Rica/ Panama grows larger

SOUTH AMERICA

⊢⊤⊢ Fault line

+⊢+ Collision line

21 Million Years Ago

Atlantic Ocean

N&S Hispaniola start to collide

CUBA

PUERTO RICO

JAMAICA (submerged)

SOUTH HISPANIOLA (part submerged)

Lesser Antilles appear as small volcanic islands

Land Bridge

Now large islands are almost contiguous

Last gap (Panama passage)

SOUTH AMERICA

and differences in fossils, and living creatures. The following froggy story, told in instalments throughout this book, is based largely on the work of Blair Hedges.

The frogs are thought to have come originally from South America. They must have moved from there up the proto-Antilles island chain around seventy to 80 million years ago. As the ancestral frogs were moving north, the islands were still forming and being scrunched and squeezed between North and South America. So connections would have been made and broken many times between the changing islands. The frogs may have been the first passengers of the island 'arks', for they were already on board when the islands were berthed in the Yucatán. They disembarked and established a foothold on the continent, which today has expanded to 68 species ranging south from Mexico. This reversal of stowaways, more a jumping ship, is evidence of the connection along the island chain, from South to North America. Not all *Eleutherodactylus* frogs jumped off, many stayed, and today there are 139 species found on the islands of the Greater Antilles, from Cuba to Puerto Rico. How they moved around the islands is a story told later in this book. Did anything board from North America?

Caribbean pines

These are possible candidates. They are a very ancient group of trees, far older than the showier flowering plants. Their branches could have supported the nests of *Archaeopteryx*, and their deep shade would have protected the dinosaurs from the strong Jurassic sun. Over their long history, pines have found their way into most parts of the world. The North American continent is particularly well endowed with species of pines, and Mexico has the greatest number of species of any country in the world. It is likely that pines boarded the rocky Caribbean cruisers from the north.

Why are Caribbean pines likely to have been early passengers? They have no real means of getting their seeds across hundreds of kilometres of salt water and they were present when the Caribbean islands were brushing against North America. Caribbean pines have heavy seeds that would naturally fall straight to the ground. The plant's strategy, however, is to drop its seeds on to freshly-burnt ground. A passing forest fire leaves the ground bare and fertilized with the ashes of plants that might otherwise have out-competed the seeds for light and nutrients. The woody cones hold the seeds secure and safe from the transitory high temperatures. They are designed to open slowly with the heat, releasing the seeds after the fire has past by. The new generation of seedlings springs up around their mothers. Eighty million years ago one generation of pines may have sprouted on the soil of the docked islands.

How long have butterflies been on earth?

It is hard to conceive a world without butterflies. They are so gorgeously coloured, so fragile and balletic in flight, that most of us never get over our initial amazement and ask questions such as when did they first grace the skies? The answer lies in the fossil record.

Unfortunately less than 40 butterfly fossils have ever been found. This is not surprising when we consider how delicate they are. Few butterflies receive a suitable burial, fewer still are preserved in solid rock, and only a tiny proportion are found by keen-eyed geologists. The few precious fossils show the butterflies to be an ancient group of creatures, very conservative in body-plan and design. Butterflies have changed little in their looks since they first appeared in the Cretaceous world (144 to 66 million years ago), when they may well have dazzled dinosaurs, such as *Dilophosaurus*, with their beauty. It is likely that the butterflies arose at about the same time as the angiosperms, the flowering plants. This would make sense as butterflies and plants depend so much on each other. The flowering plants produce showy blossoms and nectar to entice and reward the butterflies, and the butterflies, in turn, pollinate the plants, acting as sexual go-betweens. The Cretaceous world must have been very colourful as more and more blossoms and butterflies evolved and filled the world with their vibrant hues.

Butterflies, as a group, are old enough to have been on the passenger-list for that very first Caribbean cruise. What evidence can we provide for that? The longer a butterfly, or any other creature for that matter, remains on an island, the more likely it is to evolve into a unique island form, an endemic species, different from its continental ancestor. Over half the butterflies of the West Indies are endemic, so many appear to have been on the islands a long time. What other facts point to the butterflies being among the original passengers? First an obvious question needs to be addressed. As butterflies have wings why should any have needed the assistance of mobile islands? The answer depends on the individual species. Most butterflies are reasonable flyers - some like the Monarch are famous for their long-distance migrations - but others are poor aviators, capable of only short fluttery flights. There are butterflies on the Greater Antilles that are among the least likely to have arrived by their own powered flight.

Dismorphia is a genus of pierid butterflies found on Cuba, Hispaniola and Puerto Rico. It is related to the dread 'cabbage white' and its clan, but *Dismorphia* is a very unusual pierid genus. Firstly, it is not white but a beautifully marked orange and black. Moreover, the two species are poor flyers. The butterflies live in the forest and are very sedentary. *Dismorphia spio* is quite common on Puerto Rico, but has never been found on the islets just a few hundred metres offshore. What chance of its ancestor having flown 1000 kilometres from the mainland?

Ithomiidae (glasswings) are even more feeble flyers than *Dismorphia*, moving no more than a few metres in an average lifetime. They live in the depths of the forests. The patterns on their transparent wings, and the lack of colour make them very hard to see. There are two species in the Caribbean, *Greta diaphana*, and *Greta cubana*. As it is difficult to conceive of them surviving a flight of a few hundred metres away from the calm air of their dark forest world, never mind a marathon flight over open water, they are very strong candidates for having travelled out with the islands. The distribution of the butterflies certainly adds to the other evidence, from frogs and pines, that the islands acted as 'Noah's Arks'.

Islands setting sail

The Caribbean plate never stopped moving during the period that the islands collected their living cargo. What happened was that the northerly islands, in particular Cuba, brushed against the continent as they moved eastward. After a period of around 20 million years the land connection was severed, and the islands continued to move north-eastward. This casting off from the North American dockside was made more dramatic by the very high sea levels at the time. Much of Cuba, the nearest island, was under water.

Tiny todies

The todies are a family of birds found nowhere else on earth. There are many unique species of animals in the Caribbean, but this is an endemic family, and a family of birds at that. At first sight, birds would seem to be obvious candidates for travelling to islands under their own power. But todies are very small, and not noted for their powerful flight. They do not migrate, or fly long distances. On the contrary, they are strongly territorial, real 'stay-at-homes'. As they also tend to skulk, low down in forests, sheltered by the trees, it is dubious that they would have been blown across water by gales. Part of an ancient lineage of birds, it is highly likely that their ancestor would have been part of the scene when the Antilles 'set sail'. A 30-million-year-old fossil of a tody has been unearthed in Wyoming. So, they could well have joined the islands early in their voyage eastward; though we may never be able to say with total confidence how these cute bundles of feathers arrived. There is one species of tody on each of the Greater Antillean islands, except for Hispaniola, but an explanation for that idiosyncrasy is given later. Each island has a different species. The ancestral tody may well have flown the short distance from North America to join Cuba, the nearest island of the cruise fleet, and then hopped (or fluttered) down the flotilla to the other islands.

The Cuban glasswing butterfly. No great aviator, it is a ghostly presence of the dark forest floor.

These curious, dumpy, brilliantly-plumaged birds are distantly related to the kingfishers, which are found worldwide, but have most species in Asia, Australia and New Guinea. The closest relatives to the todies are the motmots and jacamars, and, like their mainland relatives, the todies are insect-eaters. Their technique is to perch and search. The bird sits motionless; or, bill tilted upwards in a characteristic posture, merely twists or tilts its head to scan for 'bugs'. Once a potential prey has been sighted the tody launches into space. The bird typically flies upwards and grasps its prey from twigs or from under leaves. The prey, sometimes a large insect, such as a wasp or cricket, is held in the bill while the bird flies back to a perch. The tody prepares its meal by beating it against the branch, before swallowing. The purpose of this action may be to tenderize the large beakfull and make it easier to swallow, or it may remove the sting from the abdomen of a wasp. The todies were among the first vertebrates to prey on the hordes of insects on the islands. But it is probable that there was another insectivore 'passenger' that was as bizarre in appearance as the tody is cute.

The bizarre *Solenodon*

These are real oddball mammals. They look like large shrews, and have the air of scruffy, poorly put-together animals, with long snouts, curious bare legs and tiny eyes. The *Solenodon's* ancestors are known from fossils found in rocks in North America which date back 55 to 60 million years ago. The fossils give the *Solenodon* an ancient pedigree, particularly for a mammal. Most mammals just weren't around when the islands set out on their voyage. The majority of mammals evolved after the 'ships' set sail. They could not have been passengers. The *Solenodon* is a primitive insectivore that was most likely widespread in North America when dinosaurs still ruled the earth. Today there are just two, or perhaps three species, *Solenodon cubanus* found only in eastern Cuba and *Solenodon paradoxus* from Hispaniola. The third species is *Solenodon marcanoi* from Hispaniola, which may or may not be extinct. Their mainland ancestors died out long ago, perhaps out-competed by more modern mammals. The odd distribution may reflect the ancestral animal arriving just around the time the islands left their North American 'harbour'. They either walked aboard, swam the short distance from shore, or, more believably, drifted over aboard a raft. Once on the shifting island of Cuba they stowed away, and later moved down the mobile chain as far as Hispaniola. Little is known of these creatures. They are nocturnal and rare. The small body of information that we have has been gleaned from captive animals.

There is some evidence that *Solenodons* have a few rather unusual traits. It appears that they use ultrasound to communicate with each other. More unusual is the suggestion that they use poison. Their teeth, small and sharp like most insectivores, have grooves running down them. These grooves are thought to transport poison to the captured prey. The female normally gives birth to one or two young. The natural society for *Solenodons* seems to be a maximum of two or three, composed of a mother and her offspring. The young are transported for the first six weeks by clamping on to the mother's teat and being dragged along. This mode of movement, unique in insectivores, may allow the female to forage unhindered by her babies. Even at 75 days of age, the youngsters will still run alongside their mother, holding tightly to the teats. The *Solenodon* still graces the Caribbean islands, a 'relic' of an earlier age. It survives in its isolation, freed from the fiercer competition on the mainland that appears to have driven its relatives over the brink and into the abyss of extinction.

The Bob Geldof of mammals? A juvenile *Solenodon*: the charm of the animal lies in its oddball appearance.

The asteroid

The evidence for stowaways on board the moving islands is strong, but, considering the number of other potential passengers, why did so few board? It is a difficult question to answer. Maybe lots did and then became extinct. If so, where are the fossils? On the other hand, perhaps the high sea levels at the time meant that the islands were far removed from any dry land on the North American continent. Recently a powerful new reason for the low numbers of living descendants of the first passengers has come to light. In 1979, Walter Alvarez and his father, Luis, published a scientific paper that created a whirlwind of debate. What they suggested was that an asteroid had collided with the earth 65 million years ago. Some scientists now believe the object was more likely to have been a comet. The time of the asteroid or comet collision coincided with the extinction of the dinosaurs. The suggestion was that the extra-terrestrial body had led to the demise of the dinosaurs (and much else besides).

A comet travels through space at a colossal 200 000 kilometres an hour. The whole cataclysmic event would have been over in a few seconds. The comet's surface heated up, glowing white hot, as it entered the earth's atmosphere and punched into the planet. The violence of such a high-velocity impact vaporized the comet. Ten times the missile's mass of surrounding rock was atomized in the same instant. The blast was the equivalent of detonating the world's atomic arsenal 1000 times. The initial result was a hole 160 kilometres across and 40 kilometres deep in the earth's crust. But the trouble was only just beginning. The dust and debris was ejected at 50 times the speed of sound. A fireball lofted 1500 cubic kilometres of material straight up into the highest layers of the atmosphere. (Mount St Helen's managed to burp out a meagre 1.3 cubic kilometres of volcanic ash.) The sun was blotted out for several months, with little or no sunlight, photosynthesis was impossible. The temperature dropped, long enough perhaps to eliminate the most famous casualties, the dinosaurs. Acid rain deluged the blighted planet. The acid rain may well have killed the marine plankton. If some of the vaporized rock was limestone, then vast amounts of carbon dioxide would have produced a blanket that drove up the global temperatures for centuries. These are the global effects. Near to the point of impact, ground zero, things were much worse! Twenty-thousand cubic kilometres of melted mangled rock was thrown out sideways, landing within a radius of 5000 kilometres. This 'local' rain of rock was not the end of the horror story. A marine impact would have produced huge waves, as high as four kilometres. These cloud-high giant breakers would have raced out from the impact.

The impact site is now agreed to be in the Caribbean: the most favoured location being the Yucatán Peninsula, which, at that time, would have been submerged under a shallow sea. Cuba and Hispaniola were the nearest land masses. The giant waves would have still been over half a kilometre high when they reached the coastline. The result is predictable: mass destruction. It is hard to conceive of anything surviving the colossal waves, which would have completely scoured low-lying islands, ripping up house-sized rocks and carrying them miles, before depositing them like strand-line flotsam. The walls of water washing over hillsides would have smashed everything in their path.

The asteroid or comet that may have killed the dinosaurs could well have been responsible, too, for the low passenger numbers on the initial part of the voyage. Few plants or animals could have survived the tsunamis (tidal waves). There is an interesting speculation that the frogs, fish and birds survived because many of them are highland beasts. They may have lived above the tide-line of the monster waves. If so, what a vision these creatures would have witnessed: the tsunami rolling inexorably towards the islands, sweeping over the lowlands and crashing up against the steep volcanic mountainsides. The glaring gaps on the passenger list are for lowland amphibians. While there are many frogs in the West Indies, there are no members of the other two major groups of amphibians, the salamanders and caecilians (legless, worm-like subterranean beasties). These groups, typically, are found in the lowlands.

The Caribbean shuffle

The eastward motion of the Caribbean plate continued. There was a problem though - the Bahamas. Around 55 million years ago Cuba ran into the Bahamas bank, a huge platform of limestone, and was stopped in its tracks. The northern half of Cuba is composed of the limestone from the Bahamas bank. Only the southern half is the original travelling island. The weld line runs down the centre of modern Cuba. The grounded Cuba brought subduction to a halt in the Greater Antilles. The rest of the Caribbean plate, with its vanguard of islands, kept moving east. The result was a mess. Cuba was stretched and sheared, as other islands scraped past. The shear broke the early Caribbean islands into their parts and began to define the outlines of modern Cuba, Hispaniola and Puerto Rico. As a new fault line appeared to the south of Cuba, allowing the other islands to continue their journey eastward, the largest island in the Caribbean was left behind. The exact location of the fault line changed over time, so that bits of some islands slipped up to each other to form new larger islands. Other islands were ripped apart and the pieces slid along the fault line to new locations. Puerto Rico was separated from Hispaniola and moved 350 kilometres east in this fashion, starting about 35 million years ago. A further 12 million years later another fault line appeared between Cuba and Hispaniola, dragging Hispaniola east. Up until then, Cuba and

The big crunch. An asteroid collides with the earth,
punching a hole in the atmosphere and creating a colossal tidal wave.

Hispaniola had been one larger island. The total distance of eastward slippage since Cuba ground to a halt has been over 1000 kilometres.

What about the fish?

Fish may seem a strange group of animals to turn to for evidence of ancient land-connections between the islands. Surely they could swim out to the islands? The answer is yes and no. As was mentioned earlier, there are freshwater fish, such as the lungfish, that would die if forced to swim in the ocean because sea water is too salty. Marine fish are designed to maintain the balance between a saltier sea and their less salty bodies; freshwater fish have the opposite problem, and have a 'salt pump' that actively keeps their bodies more salty than the sweet water they live in. Put a freshwater fish in the sea and its design works against it, trying to keep its body saltier than the sea. This business of 'salt pumps' is true for purely freshwater and marine fish, but there are fish that have evolved a tolerance to variations in the saltiness of water. In this category are freshwater fish that can survive brackish water. All the 71 species of freshwater fish in the West Indies are of this more tolerant type.

This suggests that the ancestors of today's Caribbean fishes did swim to the

The cave fish of Cuba. These bizarre creatures live in absolute darkness, prowling the labyrinthine rock-lined streams deep below the surface of Cuba's limestone country. They are little studied!

islands, but not the hundreds of kilometres across the open sea. Most Caribbean fish are a few centimetres long, hardly the strong long-distance swimmers able to make the journey. Perhaps there is some other way that the fishes arrived on the Antilles? There is a scenario, which must remain speculative (for there is only one fossil of a fish from the whole of the Greater Antilles), and which supports the plate-tectonics history of the Caribbean.

The majority of the Caribbean fish are perfectly at home on the margins of the land and sea, in mangroves and lagoons as well as freshwater ponds and streams. Many are unusual, among fishes, in that they give birth to live young able to cope with the stresses of changing salinity and temperature of swamps, rather than laying eggs that are unlikely to hatch.

Might these tough little fish have swum the shorter distance to the islands when they were berthed against North America? This is possible, though difficult to prove one way or another. The pattern of distribution of the fishes suggests that they may have migrated along the proto-Caribbean islands when they were close to the continent, and more closely connected together. The greatest variety of fishes occurs on Cuba, which has 28 species from nine different families. There are more fish in western than eastern Cuba and the diversity further decreases as you move down the islands with Hispaniola, next in line, possessing only four families of fish, but 32 species, and last and definitely least, Puerto Rico with no endemic freshwater fish at all. This decrease in the number and variety of species fits the movement of the ancestral fish down the line of the islands, because the further from the mainland, the less species would be expected. If the fish moved through the brackish coastal lagoons and swamps, that would explain the lack of true freshwater fish. The low-lying marshes and the shallow salt water that connected the islands would be no barrier to the salt-tolerant ancestors of today's fish.

Why are there no freshwater fish on Puerto Rico? If the fish, moving down the line of closely connected islands, arrived at Puerto Rico *after* 35 million years ago, they may have 'missed the boat'. Puerto Rico, the 'boat' at 'the end of the jetty', had cast off from the end of Hispaniola around then. The fishes may not have progressed that far down the islands. They must have colonized both Cuba and Hispaniola, before the latter island slid away 12 million years later. Hispaniola, being further from the continent, had only a few fish species, and none of the spectacularly weird-looking cave fishes of Cuba, nor the antique gar fish. It did have the ancestor of the *Poeciliidae*, a family of live-bearers. Once Hispaniola had moved off east, this small fish essentially had the island to itself, and it evolved to fill all the different habitats: mountain streams, lowland ponds, super-salty lakes, mangroves, even a hot sulphurous spring. There are now 28 species of *Poeciliidae* and they dominate Hispaniola's waters.

Tree-dwelling frogs

As the islands split up, so the frogs were isolated and formed groups. The frogs that live on Puerto Rico and Hispaniola today are tree-dwellers. This is probably their original way of life, and this group may represent the original inhabitants of the drifting islands.

On Puerto Rico, the Luquillo Mountains are the last large expanse of rainforest. This is home to several species of frogs. As the last light of a summer's day fades behind the distant forested ridge, the expected tranquillity of a tropical evening is short-lived. The Luquillo forest becomes ear-splittingly noisy as tens-of-thousands of frogs advertize their presence in the fading light.

The most numerous and largest - a veritable giant at five centimetres long - is called the coqui, after the sound of its dominating call *co-qui*. Like other members of this huge group, coquis lay a few large eggs. The spherical walls of the egg are the outer limits of the tadpoles' universe until they metamorphose and hatch as miniature adults. The males guard the eggs, which are hidden in curled-up leaves, or under the bark of trees. The coqui's claim to fame is not its gigantic size, but its curious nocturnal journeys. Just after dusk, and particularly after rains, coqui frogs emerge from their daytime refuges in the lower branches and climb up the tree trunks into the canopy. Here, there are many more small insects to feed upon than down below. The canopy is multi-layered, and each level of leaves and branches has its own infestation of 'bugs'. It is this architectural complexity that leads to the canopy having many more insects than the ground below. Ironically, many of the insects high in the tree tops have been blown up there from the ground vegetation of forest clearings. While the canopy is rich in insects, it is also windy. The wind is a killer to the moist thin-skinned amphibians, which quickly dehydrate. The reason frogs are largely nocturnal is to avoid the danger of dehydration.

The timing of the frogs' climb to the food-rich forest canopy is very precise. They must emerge in the relatively cool humid conditions of night, but if they leave it too late, then they may be ambushed by nocturnal predators. The predators appear after 7.30 p.m., so it is not surprising that the coquis' rush-hour is from 7 p.m. to 7.30 p.m. Then, after a night of feasting in the canopy, the frogs must descend before dawn to avoid the tropical sun and the strong winds of daytime. They now play their ace card: instead of lumbering down the trunk, they parachute to the ground, saving precious energy. The fall may be as much as 15 metres, an immense drop for a small frog. They spread their feet and splay their fingers and toes to control their descent, and speed of fall. In mid-air they look like miniature free-falling human parachutists. Beginning at 5 a.m., the coquis all descend at the same time creating a gentle patter of falling frogs, which, as dawn approaches, turns into a shower and then into a rain of frogs. Once on the ground the frogs soak up the early-morning dew, replenishing their precious fluids. Fed and watered, they return to their crevices in the lower storey of the trees, to hide out for the day. This spectacular means of making a living may have gone on for millions of years in the forests of Puerto Rico.

The travelling islands

Once the islands had travelled a good distance out from the lee of the North American continent, then the only way land plants and animals could get aboard was by long journeys on rafts. This would certainly have been the case by 45 million years ago, probably a lot earlier. The late arrivals for the Caribbean cruise would have had to find their own way to join the original passengers. Is there evidence for all this shuffling of species, apart from the distribution of the descendants living today? Although there are few fully fossilized remains of plants or animals, there is evidence of their ancient presence in the Caribbean. It comes from an exquisitely beautiful source: amber.

CHAPTER 3

JOINING THE CRUISE

One humid, sticky summer day, 30 to 40 million years ago, the increasing sound of rustling leaves in the forest canopy signalled the coming storm. The wind built up in the afternoon, and by the evening the sky was illuminated by numerous electrical storms all along the coastline of the island of Hispaniola. Building and building throughout the night, the wind reached hurricane force, ripping up small trees and tearing limbs off the forest giants growing along the numerous streams of the coastal lowlands. Waves whipped up into mobile mountains of water. The sea level rose ten metres and the angry grey waves swept over the low-lying land, carrying away much of the litter. Snapped by the storm, broken branches exuded sticky sap, which sank into the neighbouring coastal lagoons along with the saturated wood. The process of making amber had begun. A fossilized tree sap, amber is now mined in the northern mountains of the Dominican Republic, the eastern half of the island of Hispaniola.

The *Hymenaea* tree's sap is a defence against its numerous insect-attackers, and the *Hymenaea* species in the Amazon can produce metre-long stalactites of sap in their battle to ward off wood-boring beetles, and to seal entry holes from further attack. The sap contains turpenes, powerful chemicals which can prevent fungal infestation, and deter injurious insects. Modern-day *Hymenaea* trees are large and very generous producers of sap, and there is little doubt that the trees on Hispaniola, 30 million years ago, were equally productive.

Trapping all in its path as it dribbled down the injured branch or trunk, the sticky sap entombed a large array of insects, and, today, that amber is a window into the world of Hispaniola 30 to 40 million years ago. Inside its golden globs lies a miniature menagerie. There are beetles and termites that lived on and inside the decaying wood of the tree, flowers and leaves of *Hymenaea*, rootlets of orchids and pieces of moss that must have fallen from the higher branches of the tree, and diving beetles trapped during their night-time flights from pond to pond. Ants are also common, with more than 40 species discovered, and stingless bees that were trapped when they were collecting the sap to construct their nests. Assassin bugs are also over-represented in the amber, for they hunted alongside the ribbons of resin. There are even mushrooms, a pseudo-scorpion in the act of hitching a lift on the leg of a beetle, and adult mosquitoes that specialize in breeding in bromeliads that presumably lived on the branches of the *Hymenaea* tree (see the Jamaican bromeliad story in this chapter). The most precious inclusions in the amber are vertebrates. There is an *Eleutherodactylus* frog, perhaps drawn to the sap

PREVIOUS PAGES: The Blue Mountains of Jamaica. These forested slopes are the home of many unique plants and animals, including the bromeliad crab.

by the prospect of an easy insect meal. There are a few bird feathers that may have drifted down from a preening woodpecker perched above the oozing sap, thirty million years ago. Lizards and geckos are occasionally found, but these are very rare. There are records of only seven frogs, six geckos, four *Anolis* lizards (or anoles) and three bird feathers from all the years of mining and collecting Dominican amber. Not surprisingly, there are no mammals trapped in the amber, but the fossil sap does hold evidence of their presence: there are embedded mosquitoes and ticks, horseflies and fleas which must have fed on the blood of mammals. The best proof is an embedded tick still clutching on to the hairs of its warm-blooded host.

The amber from the Dominican Republic is the source of bacteria now flourishing in a laboratory in California. Celebrating their 25 millionth birthday, the bacteria were 'revived' by two scientists at the California Polytechnic State University. This extraordinary business out-does the science fiction of *Jurassic Park*, with scientific fact. Raul Cano and a student, Monica Borucki, cracked open a blob of amber to extract a stingless bee, one of the most common victims of entombment, and the bacteria, which had originated in the bee's gut and survived as spores for 25 million years, were removed. Bacteria commonly form spores when conditions are not ideal and amber is a relatively benign environment to wait out the aeons.

Rafts

But how did creatures, frozen forever in amber, arrive on the island? Some, like the *Eleutherodactylus* frog, came with the islands, but the great majority made their way there on rafts of floating vegetation. The chances of these enforced emigrants surviving the perils of the long sea journey must have been very slim, just as the likelihood of the raft bumping into dry land, rather than drifting out to oblivion in the Caribbean or the Atlantic Ocean, must have been minuscule. But the means of transport is not uncommon. The raft-building still goes on today, and tangled mats of vegetation travel the great Orinoco river that flows out of the highlands of Venezuela. The Orinoco is a model for other ancient rivers that must have sent out the first unknowing colonists.

Each year, with the onset of the rains, the Orinoco floods as the unbearable heat and soporific humidity of the tropics reaches an irritable crescendo at the end of the dry season. This time of year is marked by the ballooning thunderheads that appear each afternoon. Day after day they build, the air charged with electric tension; then it is all over: the skies open and huge volumes of water descend. The droplets are large and forceful, and the density of the deluge blots out everything more than a few metres away. Within hours the world is transformed, the noise of

ABOVE: A tiny *Eleutherodactylus* frog, entombed in amber for over 25 million years.

OPPOSITE: A downy feather, its delicate structure perfectly displayed
by the hardened tree resin that is fossil amber.

the rain a memory, the air clean and cool, the streets awash, the fields turned to mud. The huge tropical downpours fill the streams, overflow the lakes and marshes, saturate the soils of the floodplains, and the mighty river begins to rise. It is an amazing spectacle. In a matter of hours, the strength of the current quickens, the water becomes turbid, the level rises, and the river takes on a new character, its power grown inexorably.

The surge of fresh water hurtling down the Orinoco cuts into the outside banks of the many bends where huge forest trees, covered in a wall of intertwining vines, hang their roots into thin air. The bank erodes, large cubes of clay and sand tumble into the torrent and are instantly washed away. The trees follow soon afterwards, undercut by the current. The tangled mess that was once a stately forest giant moves down the flooded river, a vessel for the unfortunates that were living on and under its limbs and branches. Other creatures, cast into the fierce flow of the

river swim for the 'life raft'. Still others, marooned on logs and islands by the rising waters, make for the safety of the fallen tree. In the lower course of the mighty Orinoco, the current slackens, and the river dithers and splits into several courses as it forms a delta mouth. Here, the individual rafts may link to form juggernauts which issue into the Caribbean. The prevailing westerly ocean currents then tend to carry the castaways towards the islands.

The rafts might have been a risky form of transport, but most creatures were washed up on the islands by this means. Arriving over an immense period of time, multiplying by millions of years the minuscule odds of a lucky landing, the rafts brought many insects and other invertebrates, as well as the few mammals that were to evolve on the islands. The rafts, for example, ferried the ancestors of the rodents that populated the islands. Fifty-five kinds of rodents are known to have lived on the Greater Antilles, all but 13 now extinct.

A success story
Professor Hedges' work, using the 'molecular clock' of cell-protein mutation, suggests that the arrival of *Anolis* lizards – the most successful of the reptile arrivals in the Caribbean – may have spanned 20 million years. Starting around 36 million years ago there were probably several invasions, with different pioneers for each island. These lizards, ensnared by the sticky sap of a *Hymenaea* tree all those millions of years ago, could well have been the founders of a great dynasty – an explosion of the *Anolis* species. One of the ironies of island life is that the hardest part is getting there. After arriving by raft, the anoles found the island helpfully lacking in many of their competitors and predators, thus allowing them evolutionary scope for a rapid radiation of the original species into a multitude of others to fill the empty 'niches'. This resulted in 138 species scattered throughout the Caribbean – almost half the total number of species of these lizards. The rest of the anole tribe lives in Central and South America. It is a measure of the success of these reptiles that the *Anolis* genus makes up between five and ten per cent of the world's lizards. They really have radiated in a spectacular way.

The islands of the Greater Antilles have their own unique anoles. Cuba has over 40 species, with only one in common with Jamaica, and that was most likely introduced recently by humans; Jamaica has a further six endemic species; Hispaniola has more than 35 species, all unique to the island; and Puerto Rico has its very own group of 11 species. So the lizards are not Caribbean so much as Cuban or Puerto Rican. The bands of species on each island are probably the descendants of separate singular moments of stunning serendipity: the shipwreck of a raft with anoles of both sexes still alive.

For Puerto Rico, that moment happened about 15 million years ago. The lucky lizards came from Hispaniola and their descendants, the lizards on Puerto Rico today, have been studied in some detail. The anoles have evolved to exploit the opportunities that the island offered. They seem to follow six distinct 'professions' or ways of life. There are three different species in the canopy of the forest. The largest of the island's anoles is found here, along with the smallest. The 'crown giant' – an impressive and aggressive animal – can reach a length of over 30 centimetres (an old-fashioned foot). Its large head and a crest along its neck give this lizard an imperious look. The smallest member of the tribe is fully grown at 6 centimetres and is known as the twig dwarf anole. This species has short strong legs for grasping twigs, and a prehensile tail for the same reason. It tends to be well camouflaged and freezes when disturbed. Living on the outermost twigs, it is more exposed to aerial predators than its relatives, and its cryptic colour and motionless pose are defences against avian attack. The anole moves slowly, for it specializes in feeding on insects found on the most delicate, most precarious twigs and, while there, faces no competition from its larger relative. On an island full of opportunities, the twig anole has evolved to fill a similar role to that of the old-world chameleon. The third species in the tree tops is halfway between the giant and the dwarf, and so takes medium-sized insects. It also tends to stay closer to the upper sections of the trunk.

Tree trunks are a vertical highway for insect food, and this territory has been partitioned into three by the anoles. In addition to a mid-sized canopy specialist, there is a central- and a lower-trunk lizard. The lowest section of the trunk is the domain of an anole of approximately the same size as the owner of the upper trunk. Sandwiched in between the main trunk is the territory of an anole which feeds on smaller insects and does not directly compete with its immediate neighbours. The last member of this group is the ground anole that makes its living hunting among the bushes and tall grasses. These different lifestyles appear to be common to all the Greater Antillean islands.

It is not just the number of different species of anoles that strikes the visitors to these islands, the sheer sum total of individuals is staggering. They are the most visible animals in the Caribbean. Lizards are cold-blooded, or rather more accurately, they do not use the energy from food to warm themselves. Instead, they depend on the warmth of the sun. This means they require less food than the warm-blooded beasts whose place they have assumed. The difference is surprising; the food required to power one insectivorous bird would satisfy a hundred lizards. The result is that there can be a lizard for every square metre of land, and, even at densities one quarter of that, a small island of 400 square kilometres may have 100 million individuals!

The first hurricanes

Whilst the creatures of the land were conveyed by flood and ocean currents to their new island homes, the creatures of the air were carried by the most terrible of storms – the hurricane. At some point in the long process of the widening of the Atlantic, the first hurricanes must have swept out of the east to strike the Caribbean islands. Hurricanes are spawned by tropical oceans. As the seasons move from winter to summer, the sun moves north across the Equator and the seas are heated by the fierce overhead sun. Out in the Atlantic, the warm surface-waters evaporate. Clouds bubble up. The rising humid air sucks in more air, and an area of low pressure is formed. If conditions are ideal the storm continues to grow. The winds associated with the air that is drawn into the growing 'local atmospheric disturbance' are thrown into a spiral by the rotation of the earth – a tight whorl of dense white clouds. Then the tropical storm starts to move, heading west with the prevailing winds. As it tracks across the tropical seas, the spiral arms suck up more and more water-sodden air. The storm feeds off the seas, the winds grow stronger, and an eye of intense low pressure forms in the centre. A hurricane is born.

Hurricanes have an almost unimaginable violence. The winds can exceed 200 kilometres an hour. The first landfall of this fierce creation of the tropics is frequently the Caribbean islands, which have long been known as 'hurricane alley'. The winds smash trees, draw up the seas to flood the low-lying coastal fringes and, as the storm moves on, it carries leaves, seeds and many birds caught in its path of destruction. When the hurricane moves over land it is cut off from its source of power – warm water – and it loses its strength, sense of direction and starts wandering aimlessly. If the path of the hurricane meanders from mainland to the islands, or from island to island, then it may act as a conveyor-belt in the sky, delivering its involuntary passengers to new lands.

Cuban birds

Cuba is home to many endemic species of birds. Some are such poor fliers that they were likely to have been carried by the wild winds. There is a wren that lives only in the Zapata swamps, close to the infamous Bay of Pigs. It shares the vast swamp with the Zapata rail, another species found nowhere else on earth. Both these species merit the birders' abbreviation, LBJ – little brown jobs. But the birds of the Greater Antilles have among their number some of the most spectacular creatures on earth. The Cuban trogon is one such animal and it lives in the

A hurricane as seen from a space shuttle. The eye of the storm is clearly visible.

woodlands that fringe the Zapata swamps. The bird has a mournful, evocative, frequently repeated call which makes it easy to locate. Once seen, the bird is never forgotten; it is gorgeously bedecked in feathers of red, blue and green. These are the colours of the Cuban flag, and the trogon is the national bird. But even the trogon is outshone by its diminutive neighbour, the Cuban bee hummingbird. This is aptly named, for it is little bigger than a bumble-bee and is the smallest bird on earth. The male is not just the smallest of birds, it is one of the most brilliant. The whole head is bright iridescent red.

This species is confined to the island of Cuba and its small southern satellite, Isla de Juventud (formerly known as the Isle of Pines). The bee hummingbird is not a common bird, but it can be found in the dry woodlands that grow on the limestone surrounding the Zapata swamp.

The male spends a great deal of time perched as high as 20 metres in the tree tops looking for intruders into its territory, a tiny dark silhouette against a blue sky. The most startling transformation occurs, though, as the bird turns its head. For as the feathers on the head catch the sunlight they glow an incandescent red, and the bird becomes a living fireball. The male will aggressively fly out to meet any other male that encroaches into his airspace. There often follows a dramatic aerial chase, as exciting as any dog-fight, as the two birds, only centimetres apart, twist and turn through the complex three-dimensional obstacles of twigs and branches. The birds fly at speeds as great as 80 kilometres an hour.

The Cuban bee hummingbird, like all the hummingbirds of the Greater Antilles, came from Central America. Its ancestor was probably closely related to the fork-tailed emerald that today lives in nearby Yucatán. How did the ancestor of this diminutive bird arrive in Cuba? There is no hard evidence to help us, but it is likely that it was the victim of storms some time in the last two million years. The wind-battered 'emerald ancestors' established an island dynasty on Cuba. Many generations later this genetic line of birds evolved into the bee hummingbird. Equally spectacular was the Cuban macaw, *Ara tricolor*, now sadly extinct and known from only five specimens. This macaw is considered by some to have been the most beautiful of all the big parrots. That, considering its lovely relatives that still grace the skies of Central America, is quite a claim.

Jamaica alone

Jamaica was always the odd island out, the tail-end in the line of 'Noah's arks' cruising east. This meant that there was little exchange of living cargo during the 'journey'. Jamaica was left behind, still stuck on to the west face of Yucatán, when the other islands were breaking up and coalescing in the eastern Caribbean. By way of contrast, Jamaica was close to North America for longer than any of the other islands (other than the southern part of Hispaniola).

Thirty million years ago, Jamaica slipped away from the lee of Central America. For the last ten million years that it was docked, Jamaica was more a submarine than a Noah's ark, setting sail underwater and emerging above the sea as recently as 20 to 25 million years ago (though some argue that the Blue Mountains kept their heads above water for the whole voyage out into the Caribbean). The fact that Jamaica surfaced so recently in the time-scale of the island's epic voyage means that all Jamaica's plants and animals must have arrived there, wafted by currents of air, or rafted on currents of the sea. Jamaica's different sailing route and timetable has led to a very distinct flora and fauna.

One specific effect of the submergence period is that much of Jamaica is covered in limestone. This rock was laid down undersea. Limestone is composed of the compressed shelly bodies of marine creatures. What is important about limestone for Jamaica is that there is little surface water in those areas covered by this rock. Limestone dissolves readily in water, and, in an area of substantial rainfall, the rock soon becomes peppered with holes. The caves, caverns, crevices and shafts swallow up the water. This gives a curiously paradoxical nature to the land, for, despite the often torrential rain, giant cacti grow in some areas, giving the place the look of a desert, not a rainforest. The scarcity of surface water has led to some most intriguing adaptations. Jamaica has 784 species of flowering plants that are unique to the island. This is a heritage of Jamaica's isolation, and late appearance above the waves.

Bromeliads – the 'green star' of Jamaica

There is a great profusion of bromeliads on Jamaica and many are unique to the island. Among those found only on Jamaica are the *Aechmeas*, and 15 of the 16 (the odd one out is found on Cuba) species of *Hohenbergia* – giants of the bromeliad world. Some are over two metres across. While many live on the bare limestone ground, others bedeck the limbs of the large cloud-forest trees, creating gardens in the sky.

The bromeliad is a brilliant example of natural design. The plant is anchored to the tree limb by its roots, but gains no sustenance from its host. This is not a parasitic relationship, the bromeliad fends for itself. Like all green plants it needs minerals and water. The elegant symmetry of the plant and its long blade-like leaves are what make it attractive to us, but the real purpose of the leaves is to answer the bromeliad's needs. Rain lands on the leaves and runs down the slightly concave upper surface (no chance of water escaping over the edge). At the base of the gutter-like leaves there is a deep pocket where the water collects and is stored. The plant effectively gathers water from

ABOVE: The smallest bird in the world at only
5 cm, the Cuban bee hummingbird
is a living fireball.

RIGHT: The Cuban trogon. The national bird
of Cuba, it is found nowhere else on earth.
Its beautiful colours and mournful call
make it unforgettable.

OPPOSITE: The doctorbird, a common bird
in Jamaica, is one of the most stunning of all
hummingbirds. It drinks the nectar of bromeliads
and so provides a pollination service.

all over its surface area and funnels the precious liquid into the central reservoirs. The impounded water sustains the plant between showers. The bromeliad is a pond in mid-air!

Bromeliads are in greatest profusion in the cloud forests of the Blue Mountains. Here, even when there are long periods between rains, there is the ever-present mist. The mountains act as a barrier to the warm wet air that blows in from off the sea. As the air rises up the verdant mountainsides, the clouds condense and blanket the steep slopes before they swirl over the summits. The bromeliads have evolved a way to benefit from the damp air – they have spines running along the edges of their leaves, which act as condensers gleaning water from the enveloping mist. The freshly-formed droplets then run down the leaves. The plant must also gather nutrients, essential minerals, needed for growth. It does this in a similarly ingenious manner. The leaf surfaces are not only concave, they are very smooth. The falling cast-off leaves of the host tree are intercepted by the bromeliad's spreading foliage and funnelled down into the water at the base. Here, they rot and mulch down to make good compost.

The bromeliad's flowers are showy shades of red and purple. They are carried on tall spikes and produce copious but watery nectar. The plant needs the best pollination service. In the cool damp conditions that are typical of the cloud forest, insects are often too cold to fly. This makes them unreliable partners. Warm-blooded hummingbirds are the preferred pollinator, and the mass of reddish flowers is the visual attraction. The doctorbird – a big handsome bird, arguably the most gorgeous member of a fabulously beautiful family – is a frequent visitor to the aerial gardens. It is unlike any other hummingbird, and still puzzles scientists as to its ancestors and relatives. One thing is certain, it evolved on the island of Jamaica, for the male's tail-streamers would have been an impossible impediment to any long-distance flight from Central America.

Bromeliad crab

The bromeliads are home to a very strange assortment of creatures – a miniature world that lives within these aerial gardens and ponds. Frogs and their tadpoles are common inhabitants, as are scorpions and blue worms that live in the soil that accumulates at the base of the oldest outer leaves. Perhaps the most unusual inhabitant is the bromeliad crab, which is unique to Jamaica, and singular in other ways too. The crabs are small, growing no bigger than 20 millimetres across the shell, yet these tiny dainty-looking creatures find their way into the bromeliad gardens 20 metres or more up in the air. They seem to prefer the giant *Hohenbergia* and *Aechmea* bromeliads. These large plants can hold litres of water, and it is into these ponds in the sky that the crabs settle. The crabs pick the biggest bromeliads and, even among these, the ones that hold most water are selected.

Male and female bromeliad crabs are sedentary and, for most of the year, live apart in separate plants. But in January or February the males leave the security of their home and go courting. The females spawn at the same time and carry the 80 or so fertilized eggs underslung in their shells. The bromeliad crab now reveals its true nature. The female crab is a great mother. She battles with the constant rain of falling leaves. Against the bromeliad's best interests, the breeding female spends each night throwing out any leaves that land in her 'nursery' pool. The leaves, which are fertilizer to the plant, are a problem for the crab. The humic acid, created by the decomposing leaf, increases the acidity of the water to levels that would be dangerous to the crab's eggs and larvae. So, each night, the crab wages war, trying to subvert the action of its green host. In addition to its leaf-tossing activities, the female crab brings snails and shells into the pool to buffer the water chemistry. The shells release calcium into the water which is critical for the proper growth of the young. Without the female's activities to improve the water quality, the young would not survive.

After ten to twelve weeks the eggs hatch out in the carefully prepared pool around which the female actively pumps the water to increase the circulation and oxygen. The mother crab now guards her young against the many predators that share her bromeliad world. During the daylight hours there are two species of *Anolis* lizards that are known to feed on baby crabs, while at night there is a large predatory spider. Danger lurks, too, within the pools themselves. The voracious larva of one damselfly species lives only in the bromeliad pools. The female crab is a formidable and aggressive guard. She is quite able to kill invertebrate predators with her sharp-edged claws. She needs to be, since a single cohabiting damselfly nymph is quite capable of consuming the complete brood. More than an exemplary housemaid and guard, the mother crab also catches food, such as millipedes and beetles for her young, and brings it to the nursery for them. This may be because the pools in the leaf bases of bromeliads do not have enough food for the 20 to 30 young crabs. Without active provisioning by their mother the young may face starvation. Faced with the challenges of its environment, the bromeliad crab has evolved the highest degree of maternal care in the crab world. Unlike most other land crabs, which return to the sea to scatter their eggs, the bromeliad crab lives out its life in its aerial pool.

The geological history of Jamaica has shaped this extraordinary world inside a bromeliad. The limestone that was deposited for millions of years while Jamaica remained submerged has led to a shortage of water in the rainforest that now grows upon it. This, in turn, has led to creatures taking to the most reliable source of water: the leaf bases of bromeliads.

The female bromeliad crab is an excellent mother.
Here she is guarding her babies in their miniature world of a bromeliad leaf base.

The Hispaniola story

Southern Hispaniola was a separate island for much of the voyage of the island 'arks'. Far to the west of the other half of the present-day island, it had no opportunity for swapping or 'standardizing' its passengers. It started sliding eastwards along the fault line about 60 million years ago. Like Jamaica, there is a dispute as to whether the southern 'island' of Hispaniola was a submarine or an ark with its mountain tops raised above the level of the sea. Whatever the case, the greatest part of the island must have been submerged, only appearing above sea level as it approached the island of northern Hispaniola. Southern Hispaniola slipped up to, and collided with, the northern island as recently as ten million years ago. As it rubbed against the northern island of Hispaniola, the southern half crumpled and rose out of the sea. It sounds like another unlikely scenario, but there is evidence for the different origins of the two parts of the island from a remarkable range of animals.

The bromeliad giants of Jamaica, the *Aechmeas*,
are as much at home 30 metres up a tree as on the ground.

There are saltwater crocodiles living below sea level in Lake Enriquillo, far from the ocean. This strange state of affairs came about because of the clashing islands, and the crocodiles are victims of that event — captives of the collision. They were presumably minding their own business, basking on the shoreline of one or other of the islands but as these came together the seaway was pinched until all that was left was a lake of salty water, and the small group of crocodiles that had stayed faithful to their beach.

On the hillsides all around Lake Enriquillo are ancient beach lines, and outcrops of coral, signs of the recently retreated sea. The shoreline also has springs, some of sweet water and some highly sulphurous. These springs are the products of the continuing underground volcanic activity. They smell of bad eggs. The water of the lake, now being below sea level, cannot drain away. The minerals in the water entering the lake get concentrated as the water evaporates in the tropical heat, so the lake gets saltier and saltier each year. The crocodiles breed on a sandy island in the middle of the saline lake which has few predators and is ideal for laying eggs. But there is a problem. The hatchlings are not as tolerant of the super-salty water as their parents, so the mother crocodile gently picks up her babies between her huge teeth and laboriously ferries them in her mouth across the lake to freshwater springs on the far shore. It is a touching demonstration of maternal devotion. Ultimately, though, the crocodiles are doomed. The lake will continue to grow saltier and saltier, the fishes that the crocs depend upon will die out and the water will become too salty even for tough creatures such as the adult crocodiles. The lake will come to resemble the Dead Sea.

Hispaniola is dominated by the *Poeciliidae* family of freshwater fishes. They managed to arrive on the northern half of the island before it moved eastward, away from Cuba. Eight of the 12 species found only on the northern portion are from this family of fish that gives birth to babies. The southern part of the island also has twelve unique species, all from the *Poeciliidae* family. There are only three species found in both parts of the island. Lake Enriquillo is a sort of no-man's land, a low-lying corridor running between the two parts of the island. The three fish common to both parts of the island are found here, but there are others unique to this strange tectonic seam. There is one *Poeciliidae* fish here that lives only in a stinky sulphurous spring on the edge of the lake.

No other island in the Caribbean has such a clear-cut separation of its fishes into two geographical zones. The most likely scenario is that the fishes, living on the fringes of the northern island, moved across the narrow marine or brackish straits to the approaching southern island ten million years ago. They were then kept apart by the raised salinity of the forming Lake Enriquillo and, in their isolation, evolved into new species. This is supported by the fact that the northern island has both highland and lowland fish species, but the southern part has only lowland species. If lowland fish from the north island were the first colonists of the approaching southern island this would explain the curious lack of fish in the mountain streams there.

The tiny *Eleutherodactylus* frogs are found all over Hispaniola, just as they are on Cuba and Puerto Rico, but on Hispaniola there are two distinct tribes of these frogs. In the northern part there are frogs that live in the trees, like the original stowaways. They have always been on the island. But on the southern island there are ground-living frogs related to those on Cuba and Jamaica. The story goes something like this. At some point as Southern Hispaniola (and Jamaica) were moving eastward along the fault they rose above the sea. At this point if both islands were stationed off the south side of Cuba, then tiny frogs could have crossed from Cuba. The means of travel is unknown, but presumably would have been a short sea journey aboard a 'life' raft. This curious scenario explains why

Jamaica and Cuba have ground-dwelling frogs, as does Southern Hispaniola, while Northern Hispaniola and Puerto Rico have the little amphibians calling from the tree tops.

The separate origin of the two parts of the island is reflected even in the birds. All the other islands of the Greater Antilles have just one species of the tiny insectivorous tody, but Hispaniola has two, although the distribution of these birds is not clear-cut as in the fishes and frogs. The todies might be additional evidence.

Birds are more difficult to assess, because naturally they are more mobile and it is difficult to untangle passengers from active fliers. The two todies may have been on the separate islands, or, more likely, one may have moved from the north island on to the south island as that land mass loomed on the horizon around fifteen million years ago. Once the islands were one, the new south island species of tody may have rejoined its relative. They seem to have partitioned the island, not by geography, but by habitat. The broad-billed tody prefers arid areas, while the near-identical narrow-billed tody is a habitué of dense damp forest.

The last and most recent major event in the long biogeographical history of the Caribbean was the Ice Age.

The Ice Age in the Caribbean

The American crocodile has roamed, and still wanders throughout the Caribbean. At some point, a freshwater descendant evolved from this big impressive-looking, but shy, saltwater crocodile. The evidence from the molecular clock suggests this event was no more than four million years ago. It may well have been during the Ice Age, for the see-saw changes in sea level over the last million years created many new opportunities for the creatures of the Caribbean. During the cold snaps, much of the planet's water was locked up as ice around the Poles. In the Caribbean the sea level would have declined, the shoreline retreated, and large flat swampy expanses would have been common throughout the region – ideal habitat for a freshwater crocodile.

Today the Cuban croc can be found only in the Zapata swamp, though the Cuban authorities are breeding a second population in the Lanier Swamp on Isla de Juventud (Isle of Pines). This is the most restricted distribution of any crocodile in the western hemisphere. It was not always this way. When the sea level was lower, this stocky reptile ranged across the vast swamp plains that stretched out from today's Greater Antillean islands and fossil remains have been found on the Cayman Islands. This recent discovery helps answer a long-standing mystery: why were the islands called the Caymans? With a subtle change of spelling the answer is clear, the Caiman isles were once home to caimans (crocodiles).

The Cuban crocodile has the dubious distinction of being the most aggressive crocodile in the world. Unlike other crocs that will slip away at the first hint of humans, leaving only a widening circle of ripples as they dip underwater, the Cuban crocodile advances and keeps on advancing. Also, completely unlike other creatures, the Cuban crocodile leaps first and snaps later. This is a very ferocious animal.

The Cuban crocodile leaps beautifully, that is unless you happen to be a hutia, the endemic rodent that these crocs seem to relish. Hutias are shy vegetarian creatures about the size of a beaver – browsers who spend their time up in small trees and bushes. The crocodiles – whose technique is simple, effective, and thrilling to see – cruise around the swamp in search of them. Once they have found a hutia, the crocodiles slowly approach, only their eyes above water, until they are under the small tree in which the creature is feeding. As soon as they have a beady eye on the unsuspecting rodent, they launch upwards with enormous energy. An average croc can leap two metres in the air, jaws open. It is an awe-inspiring spectacle. With luck and the hard conservation work being carried out by the Cubans, this rascally reptile will survive until the next Ice Age releases it to roam the swamps of the Caribbean.

The Cuban ground sloths

The cooler drier climate of the Ice Age also favoured one of the few large mammals that made it to the Caribbean islands – the ground sloth. There were, in fact, several different kinds of these distant relatives of today's arboreal three-toed sloth. They grew large, and are described as part of the Pleistocene megafauna: the big mammals of the last Ice Age. The sloths probably swam across, but exactly when is open to question. Some believe that they hauled their tired bedraggled bodies from the sea about eight million years ago. Having arrived, they fared well, making up nearly a fifth of all the terrestrial mammals on the large islands. There were nine species on Cuba, six on Hispaniola, and one on Puerto Rico. The largest of the Caribbean ground sloths – the size of a bear – was *Megalocnus* of Cuba. The Ice Age climate would have suited it, providing more open deciduous woodlands.

The ground sloths were browsers who used their size to reach up to the lower branches of the trees scattered among the grasslands that would have predominated in the Ice Age. Their powerful front legs could pull down and break off branches that were beyond the reach of its mouth. However, the vegetarian sloth was

The Cuban crocodile, poised ready to launch its attack!

unfortunate in being the only large mammal about, because it became a highly desirable and eminently huntable source of meat for the early human inhabitants. Its remains have been found in the rubbish heaps of the first hunters.

The anoles of the British Virgin Islands

The Ice Age had the power to create new habitats and shape the future of species in a different manner. The rise and fall of the sea level changes the geography of the landscape, and this in turn influences the species found there. During the last Ice Age, the British Virgin Islands were not islands at all, but one larger island extending eastward to the most southerly of the Bahama Islands, that was inhabited by a variety of lizards. The 'flat island' was slowly inundated over the past 15 000 years. The tiny cays of the present-day British Virgin Islands are the high points of that gently undulating island. As the water rose the lizards were trapped on the diminishing isles, but not all have survived. The change in geography has selected some species above others. All the cays that have any lizards have *Anolis cristatellus*. This species appears the most adaptable to the conditions created by tiny isles. Islands that have two species of lizards always have the same two. So changes in geography induced by the Ice Age have dictated the species found on the islands.

The importance of extinction in the story of the Caribbean islands is easily underestimated. On a larger scale, sea-level changes and plate-tectonics have changed the landscape and, with each change, some species must have perished, just as others benefited.

What does the future hold?

Mobile islands, plant passengers, animal stowaways, shipwrecks and waifs on rafts – the story of the Caribbean is an extraordinary one. But it is not over yet. This is just one point in time on the long journey. The islands are still moving relative to the continents of North and South America. (In fact, the Caribbean is stationary, and the continents are moving steadily west, as the spreading centre of the mid-Atlantic ridge continues to produce new sea floor.)

The future is as strange as the past to our eyes and understanding, based as that is on the time-scale of a human life. The Caribbean plate, with the Lesser Antilles on the front edge, and the Isthmus of Panama as the rear border, will continue its motion out into the Atlantic Ocean. The Americas will be disconnected, the islands of Hispaniola and Puerto Rico will travel with the plate, leaving Cuba still fused to the Bahamas platform. The islands will finally meet the mid-Atlantic spreading centre, and swallow that. Thereafter, it is more difficult to predict what will happen. Will the whole spreading centre come to a halt? Or will the Caribbean Plate continue its voyage eastward, until the Lesser Antilles collide with the African coast?

Of course, this is millions of years away. What passengers will be part of this voyage will depend for a large part on our actions in the next few decades. Whether there is a full complement for the great transatlantic cruise, or just a skeleton crew, will be decided on our abilities to conserve the habitats, plants and animals of the islands. But that is the story of the last chapter of this book. Next, we look at the story of the other Caribbean islands, the Lesser Antilles, the paradise isles.

CHAPTER 4

THE PARADISE
ISLANDS

Around 50 million years ago, about the time that Cuba came to a full-stop against the Bahamas, there was more trouble brewing in the Caribbean. This time the volcanic show was out beyond the eastern edge of the Caribbean plate. The front line had leap-frogged forward 150 kilometres and the old line of volcanic islands sank beneath the waves to be replaced by the Lesser Antilles. The first volcanic islands were in the north. Over the next 25 million years a line of marine volcanoes arose, leading to a line of small islands, running north to south. Today these islands are a tropical paradise. Small green gems set in the warm turquoise waters of the Caribbean, they are the stuff of many people's holiday dreams. The names of the islands: St Lucia, Dominica, Martinique, Barbados and Guadeloupe conjure up opulent images of anchored yachts and *la dolce vita* suffused by soft tropical sunsets. But the islands are also home to a range of unique animals and plants, and this chapter looks at how they came to live in their earthly elysium.

The Lesser Antilles are different from their larger more northerly cousins, the Greater Antilles. These smaller volcanic islands are the leading edge of the Caribbean plate. They are younger and have never been connected to either of the continents. There was no opportunity for plants and animals to be transported by plate tectonics to these islands, and there never was a land bridge, so how *did* the natural inhabitants arrive on these 'Paradise Islands'?

Trinidad and Tobago

The mountainous islands of Trinidad and Tobago lie at the southern end of the chain of islands. These two islands are not part of the Lesser Antilles, their geological history is separate from the more northerly islands. They do, however, form the launch-pad for the creatures that travelled out into the blue yonder. While their history is very different from the other islands, Trinidad and Tobago look very similar to the Lesser Antilles and have a tropical climate with marked rainy and dry seasons. The lowlands have mangroves and beaches fringed with sea-grape, as well as deciduous and arid woods, while the well watered slopes of the mountains are clothed in the rich green of rainforest trees.

Trinidad is really an offshoot of South America. Although it is now an island, the seas dividing it from the continent are shallow. When the water of the oceans was locked up in huge ice-sheets and glaciers, the level of the sea would have been many metres lower. During the Ice Ages the present island of Trinidad

---

PREVIOUS PAGES: The ocelot is one of the many felines found in South America. It ranges as far as Trinidad, but no large mammals seem to have made the perilous sea journey to the Lesser Antilles.

would have been connected by a low-lying plain to the South American continent. This corridor was an easy route for exploring mammals who could have walked across and colonized what is today the island of Trinidad.

Tobago, the smaller sister, lies 38 kilometres to the north-east of Trinidad. It may never have been connected to Trinidad or the mainland, but the saltwater gap would have been very narrow. This history has led to the two islands having many of the natural riches of the mainland.

Trinidad has 247 species of breeding birds. This is a far greater number than any of the Lesser Antilles, and directly reflects the different geological histories of the islands. The birds of Trinidad and its smaller satellite, Tobago, are of South American origin. Many are forest birds that would have arrived with the trees themselves as they spread over the low-lying land that has since disappeared under the sea. A large number of tropical forest birds are highly specialized, and sedentary, spending their whole lives in the deep shade of the giant trees. The antbirds, antwrens and antshrikes are all in this category. They are the skulkers of the dark world of the forest floor and bushes, and some members of this curious tribe of birds are camp-followers of the dreaded army ants. They follow the ant-trails, feeding on the insects that fly up in a desperate attempt to avoid the thousands of biting jaws of the army columns. Even though the birds are weak fliers, there is no record of them having blown across to the Lesser Antilles; perhaps their secluded home in the deep forest has sheltered and saved them from the tropical storms.

Trinidad has many other kinds of birds that are found on the continent, but not on the more northerly Antilles. There are woodpeckers, a toucan, an oropendula, trogons, honeycreepers, a jacamar, bellbird and chacalaca. All interestingly are denizens of the forest.

The fish found on these islands are, like the rest of the animals, closely related to the South American mainland. There are only six species of freshwater fish, four killifishes and two swamp eels, compared to the hundreds that live in Venezuela. The species that are on the islands are freshwater fish that can tolerate brackish water, which suggests that there may not have been a river connection between the mainland and these islands; instead it is probable that these small fish crossed the land bridge, hugging the coastline and swimming through coastal swamps composed of myriad shallow lagoons, both salt- and freshwater. There were likely to be many such swamps in the low-lying land that formed the biological umbilical to Trinidad and perhaps even to Tobago.

For the freshwater fish, Tobago was the end of the line. The Lesser Antilles have no true freshwater fish. There was no way that they could cross the gap of 130 kilometres of open sea to the most southerly of the Lesser Antilles, Grenada.

Compared with the islands further north, Trinidad and Tobago are rich in mammal species. There are ocelots and peccaries, deer and monkeys – none of which is found on any of the small isolated oceanic isles of the Lesser Antilles. There is even fossil evidence of the tank-like glyptodont, an extinct distant relative of the armadillo which shares that animal's quaint appearance scaled up to gargantuan size. The glyptodont was one of the South American giants that played a part in the 'Great American Interchange' – the story of the next chapter.

Mammals are poor mariners, but the gap between Tobago and Grenada is small. The reason why so few mammals made the crossing successfully may lie more with the ocean currents. The Equatorial Current sweeps in from the Atlantic and flows past the islands, heading westward into the Caribbean. The reluctant sailors aboard their raft of tangled vegetation are likely to have been swept into the Caribbean Sea. There they could spend months swirling round with the clockwise currents, until they starved or their raft disintegrated and sank. Only the luckiest of involuntary oceanic explorers would have been washed up on the beaches of the islands to the north. Only the very hardiest of creatures could survive the long periods in the Caribbean Sea.

The Lesser Antilles

The *Anolis* lizards seem to be the most successful of pioneers. We have read how they colonized the Greater Antilles and went on to diversify into all the different

lifestyles that those islands allowed. The smaller Lesser Antilles permit less diversity, and the islands have only one or two species. The anoles floated out to sea perched upon vegetation that had been propelled out from the Orinoco delta. As we read in chapter 3 the huge river system floods frequently, sweeping away great rafts of vegetation – veritable floating islands that voyage down river and finally enter the sea. The successful disembarkation of the

LEFT: The purple honeycreeper, a small nectar- and fruit-feeding bird that is common on Trinidad, but absent from the Antilles.

OPPOSITE: The green iguana is a large imposing beast. Its fierce looks belie its vegetarian diet.

passengers of these rafts on to an island must have been a very rare event and most islands in the Lesser Antilles still have only a single species of anole. They are all much of a size, suggesting that there is an optimal size for an anole. This may be dictated by the food. On islands where there are two species, they have diverged into two sizes, partitioning out the available insect food and so reducing competition. The minimum size difference is a ratio of 1:1.3. Anything less than this appears unsustainable, presumably because the two species then compete for the same-sized insects.

The lizards also carve up the island on the basis of other attributes of the physical world. On the more southerly islands that are graced by two species of these elegant slim lizards, the two species have different preferred temperatures. The smaller species enjoys higher temperatures than the larger shade-loving species. On the northerly islands the larger lizard perches and hunts higher off the ground than its smaller relative.

The gentle green giant

The green iguana (common iguana) travels as well as the anole. This is a large vegetarian lizard that grows to over a metre in length and looks much fiercer than it is. The green iguana is found in Central and South American rainforests where it loves to rest in the branches of tall trees that spread out over water. This is

generally a clever ploy: they are up in the sunshine, where they can bask, but also where they can shuttle between shade and sun. Draped over the large limbs of branches, they have a clear view of any potential danger. If they are threatened by a predator climbing the tree, they have an excellent escape route – they simply drop off the branch and fall into the river below. Iguanas are strong swimmers and easily make their getaway.

The downside to this otherwise excellent strategy is that trees by rivers tend to get undercut and washed into the water, particularly during the annual floods. The iguanas are then unlikely to make it to the bank. Those that do not will be washed away either grimly swimming for their lives, or clinging to an uprooted tree and eventually ending up as residents of the Lesser Antilles chain. There are two species, but, unlike the anoles, they only come in one size. Every island has an iguana, but never both species. The endemic island species *Iguana delicatissima* occurs, for instance, on one island of the Guadeloupe group, while the common iguana, *Iguana iguana*, lives on another. The lizards – the 'rafters' – appear not to have spread north along the islands in a linear fashion. They did not 'island hop'. This is probably, as we have mentioned, due to the nature of the sea currents. For the birds and the bats, however, it is a different story.

Who's who of Caribbean birds

Birds can fly and one would think that they could spread easily across the sea to the islands of the Lesser Antilles, but it is not quite that simple. Many birds appear to have a 'fear of flying over water'. The distribution of birds tells us a great deal about the story of the paradise isles.

Trinidad and Tobago are the first points on the long string of jewel-like islands. They were even more closely connected to the continent in past times than they are now. They have a very rich diversity of birds. Trinidad, bigger and closer than Tobago, has approximately 200 different species of breeding land-birds. Tobago has only seventy, but that is many more than the next island to the north, Grenada, which has a mere thirty species. The birds of Trinidad and Tobago are almost wholly derived from the mainland. Only one bird from the Lesser Antilles, the Caribbean martin, breeds on Tobago; none does so on Trinidad. The traffic has been one way.

The giants of the parrot family, the macaws, are excellent flyers. They fly straight and fast over the tree tops as they move from their night-time roost to the fruiting trees that provide their sustenance. A macaw is capable of long flights, so there was no inherent difficulty for these birds to move out on to the islands. A putative ancestor would have been accustomed to flying over large expanses of water, for the Orinoco is a huge river, and its lower reaches are so wide that the far bank is often obscured by hazy water-sodden air. It is easy to imagine these magnificent birds flying out from the mainland or Trinidad and winging over the calm blue seas of the Caribbean. They must have made land in the Windward Islands on many occasions, so where are they today? They are all extinct. But we do have some details on them because they mostly disappeared in historical times. The exception is the St Croix macaw, which is known only from a tibia. It, too, vanished recently; the leg bone was found in the rubbish heap of the native people, the Taino. Was this unknown beauty a food item or a pet? We will never know, nor will its fabulous plumage bedazzle and enchant us.

There were macaws on Guadeloupe and Martinique. Guadeloupe, in fact, had two species. One, a typical, large multi-coloured *Ara*, was the victim of hunting, disappearing for ever around 1800. The other was a member of the *Anodorhynchus* genus. These birds are frequently more uniformly coloured than their flamboyant *Ara* relatives, but nonetheless they are spectacular birds. The largest parrot in the world, the hyacinthine macaw, belongs to this genus. The violet macaw of Guadeloupe was uniformly purple-blue with a yellow patch of bare skin at the base of its impressively large powerful bill. The description of the macaw from Martinique makes it very special. Unlike the other members of the *Anodorhynchus* genus, this bird had a belly of orange feathers, the rest of it a more typical deep blue. Was this a true species or some hybrid? Again we will never really know.

Why have these large parrots fared so badly? The cause of their demise may be very similar to why they are in such trouble today. Their beauty and intelligence may have made them desirable pets, just as they do now. Macaws are unusual in that they are often already absent from a forest before it is felled – the collectors beat the loggers to the dubious honour of local extermination of the birds. On top of their desirability as pets, macaws need large areas of forest in which to feed. As human influence makes its presence felt in an area, often fragmenting the forest into a patchwork of woods, none is large enough to support a population of large parrots. Lastly, macaws are big birds which need large trees for nest sites; today these tend to be chopped down for pasture, and, in the past, may have been felled or ring-barked in the process of slash-and-burn agriculture. So, through human influence, macaws disappeared from the Caribbean islands: one less piece of paradise. They may have been vulnerable to extinction in any case. Such small islands must have supported a perilously small population, prone to any disturbance and disease. The arrival of Europeans was enough to rapidly exterminate the birds. The smaller parrots fared a little better: the majority are at least still fighting to survive.

The parrots of today

The Amazona parrots are a delightful group of chunky medium-sized members of the family. Among their number are some of the most popular pet birds, and some fine 'talkers'. They are South American in origin. The ancestor of the Lesser Antilles species is thought to be the orange-winged Amazon, *Amazona amazonica*. Like many Amazons, this species sleeps in large communal roosts, setting out each morning to find seasonally fruiting trees.

The orange-winged Amazon is an almost ideal colonizer and founder of island species; it has so many behavioural traits that facilitate it finding an island and flourishing. It forms large flocks composed of breeding pairs and is a strong flyer that frequently covers large stretches of water as it moves from island roosts in the wide Orinoco river mouth. The birds habitually fly long distances to different areas in search of fruiting trees. The Amazons are generalists in their eating habits, so any island that a flock happened upon would almost certainly have enough food for them to thrive. No surprise, then, that parrots have been the single most successful group of Caribbean-island colonists.

There are four species of Amazons on the paradise isles, and all are now threatened. The red-necked parrot of Dominica looks most like a typical South American Amazon. The other three, from St Vincent, St Lucia and Dominica are all remarkable-looking birds and have been heavily collected in the past for parrot-fanciers in Europe and the USA. They have also suffered by the incursion of plantations into their forests. Thankfully, they are still alive and protected.

The hummingbirds

Hummingbirds are excellent colonists of islands. They are supreme aviators, the most wonderful of all winged creatures. They can fly backwards as easily as the more conventional forwards direction and are able to travel surprisingly long distances for such small birds. The rufous-tailed hummingbird of North America migrates from Mexico to Alaska and back each year, a round distance of over 6000 kilometres. These tiny avian jewels were blown or flew out on to the small islands of the Lesser Antilles at some point in the last two million years.

Trinidad and Tobago, the first 'stepping stones' out into the ocean have sixteen species of hummingbirds. These are all South American, and arrived during the Ice Age, when the lowered sea level meant the islands were connected to the continent by low-lying forest. The rufous-breasted hermit that is found on Trinidad reaches Grenada, the first island in the chain of oceanic islands that are the Lesser Antilles. The hermit is a large sedentary, dull-plumaged bird of the forest interior. It has had less opportunity to be blown off course than other more mobile hummingbirds that frequent less sheltered, windier habitats. It is found no further north, having only made it to the first 'stepping stone'.

The hermit shares its northern satellite island of Grenada with three other species of hummingbirds. All are endemic, found throughout the Lesser Antilles, and nowhere else on earth (two species are actively extending their range north-westwards into Puerto Rico). These birds – glittering jewels, their feathers predominantly green-coloured and iridescent – are more typical of hummingbirds. What separates them and how do they co-exist on such small islands? The size of the island does not seem to be important, rather it is the height of the mountains. The range of altitude offers differing habitats from humid lowland forest to highland, moss-festooned, cloud-soaked woods. In the lee of the mountains there is often a 'rain shadow' where cacti and drought-resistant deciduous trees survive. Small mountainous islands offer a greater range of vegetation and climate than larger but flatter ones. Each habitat appears to offer opportunities to newly arrived potential colonists.

The success of a colonist depends on several factors. The first is the nature of the bird. Hummingbirds, like most families of animals, can be divided into generalists and specialists. A generalist is a 'jack of all trades', able to feed from many plants with differing floral architecture, capable of catching a range of insects, and able to adapt to different physical conditions. Generalists are obviously better colonizers, quick to adapt to new relationships with plants.

The specialist hummingbird has evolved to feed at a few flowers, but to do it better than any generalist. The ultimate specialist hummingbird is the swordbill of the Andes of South America. This astounding bird has a bill longer than its body, which allows it to reach the nectar at the end of the trumpet-shaped flowers of just two plants. No other bird can feed from these plants; the bird and plant are dependent on each other for food and pollination.

Another very important factor in a colonist's success is whether the hummingbird is the first to arrive. The founder has the pick of the island. Subsequent colonists have only whatever habitat and food sources are not already utilized by the original settler. As generalists are the best invaders, they tie up a broad range of food and habitat types. What appears to happen is that the islands are divided up by altitude and flower or food size. There are often two similar - looking hummingbirds, one living in the mountains, the other down on the lowlands. The beautiful purple-throated Carib of the highlands, and its lowland relative the green-throated Carib, are a case in point. Both birds are found throughout the Lesser Antilles, and both are of similar size. They have avoided competition between themselves by living apart.

The Antillean crested hummingbird lives alongside both species of Carib. It is a tiny bird, even on a hummingbird scale, and so feeds on different flowers and insects from the Caribs. It is able to co-exist with the larger birds. Any further colonists, and there may have been many hapless arrivals over the millennia, would probably not have been able to survive. The resident generalists would have excluded them from their preferred habitats and flowers. It is likely that the islands today have the maximum number of species they can support.

The islands of the Caribbean are jewels that delight the eye, but they are also laboratories where evolutionary experiments have taken, and continue to take, place. The mammals have fared badly in these experiments. They appeared on the world scene too late to jump aboard the moving arks of the Greater Antilles, and are poor travellers over the oceans due to their need for regular and large meals. In comparison, the birds and reptiles have been successful. They have colonized many islands, arriving by diverse routes and means and have given birth to new unique species. Overall, the Greater and Lesser Antilles have few species compared to the two great continents that cradle them, but the islands are more than compensated by the beauty and uniqueness of their natural inhabitants.

CHAPTER 5

THE UNITED CONTINENTS OF AMERICA

Eighty-five million years ago, history was repeating itself as another set of explosions rent the air, 2000 kilometres out in the Pacific. The Greater Antilles had been born here 50 million years earlier. These proto-Antilles had already made their epic journey towards the continents. Another island arc was in the making with all the volcanic violence that that entailed. This new arc not only shared a Pacific birthplace with the Proto-Caribbean island arc, it set out on the same journey. Over time, the new island arc grew as the previous incarnation had, forming part of a new tectonic plate. The new chain of islands was the trailing edge of a mini plate, which had the older arc, Greater Antilles, at its eastern end. The plate was to become the Caribbean sea floor, although, at this time, it was still very definitely in the Pacific ocean. As the whole plate moved eastwards, so the new island arc was towed along, but always subducting and reworking the Pacific plate to its west.

The island arc grew in stature and length as it moved east, heading towards North and South America. Pterodons, the giants of the pterodactyl family, might have viewed the pyrotechnics as they soared on eight-metre wings. Sailing over the ocean, scanning the surface for a potential meal, they may well have fed on dead and dying fish and squid on the surface of the ocean – much as albatrosses do today. The remote islands would have given the graceful pterodons the peace and protection they needed from the numerous dinosaur predators that inhabited North America at the time.

As the islands made their slow journey towards the two American continents, they were pushing through the blue tropical waters of an ancient ocean. By 40 million years ago the Greater Antilles had cast off from the continental coasts and were 'sailing' grandly into the Caribbean. The gap between the continents was clear. An intercontinental seaway connected the Atlantic and Pacific Oceans. There was no barrier to movement of ocean currents or marine animals. This tropical seaway would have been home to an array of extraordinary creatures.

The beautiful swimmers

Blue tropical waters are still home to some of the most incredible creatures on the planet. There are no edges, no boundaries, no landmarks out in the ocean – just blue space. There is also little food. The beauty of the azure water belies its true nature. This is a savage world. Any life out here must find food with ruthless efficiency. Snails, transparent in their disguise, live in these cruel crystal-clear waters. They float in mid-water, spinning a vast mucus net. Once the construction is

PREVIOUS PAGES: The *arribada*, one of nature's great events. Thousands of female olive Ridley turtles haul themselves on to the volcanic sands of a Pacific beach in Costa Rica.

complete, the snail parachutes slowly downwards, suspended under the invisible mucus sheet. The mucus ensnares the infrequent tiny planktonic creatures. After a period of gentle decline and entrapment, the snail climbs up to the parachute. Once there, it eats the mucus sheet and the few enmeshed victims. The meagre repast over, the snail swims back to the sunlit surface waters and repeats the process.

Alongside the strange snails there would have been sea jellies (*Ctenophores*), blobs of mysterious beauty. Almost wholly composed of water, these still contrive to look the most fabulously organized of all organisms. Their bodies are really just a transparent bag in which tiny animals are digested, yet they are equipped with a variety of wondrous gadgets. Some have long, retractile sticky tentacles that ceaselessly sweep the water for plankton; others have transparent wings that control the flow of water into their 'stomachs'. They are not completely passive drifters. Their most glorious gadgets are the rows of tiny fringed plates that give them their common name of comb jellies. These combs beat in perfect time, running ripples along the side of the creature. The fringing on the comb is so fine that it splits the light, creating rainbow colours. As the creatures move, ripples of rainbow light flash down the sides of the blobs. They are like some science-fiction spaceship. The rows of combs can stop, start, and reverse instantly, so that these miniature spacecraft can change direction within their watery inner space – each change accompanied by the most glorious light show.

There are larger creatures out in this desperate marine desert. Some turtles make a living feeding on the jellies, often diving deep to feed in the black abyss. Strangest of all, though, are the warm-blooded fishes. Tuna, marlin and sailfish are formidable fleet-finned hunters. They patrol the watery desert for smaller fishes, and are able to raise the temperature of their muscles to gain greater speed through the water. The cost is larger food requirements. They appear to have adopted the riskiest of life's strategies – they are gamblers, opting to use more energy to hunt more efficiently in a sea with little food on offer. Into this strange sapphire world without edges, without surfaces, came the mobile islands. Their black volcanic sandy beaches were ideal nesting grounds for turtles.

Green turtles are the great ocean wanderers. They live in all the tropical seas of the world. There is often a distance of thousands of kilometres between their nesting beaches and feeding grounds. At some point in the past a few females chanced upon the islands during their oceanic meanderings. The beaches proved ideal for their requirements: a gentle slope, deep sand and few predators. The females laboriously laid their eggs and, eight weeks later, the young turtles emerged from the black sands and headed down the beach towards the light reflected off the sea. In some mysterious manner, the tiny turtles, some 20 to 30 years later, returned from the ocean as adults. The females laid their eggs, and so

A comb jelly reveals the marvellous intricacies of its anatomy against the black of the night sea.

confirmed the creation of a new nesting beach. The green turtles may have chanced on several ideal beaches around the shores of the mobile islands, and these nesting populations were destined to be divided by the growing islands.

Parting of the waters

The closing of the gap, the building of a barrier to marine life, happened slowly. About 20 million years ago the chain of islands was beginning to constrict the flow of water between the continents. The blockage became greater and greater as the islands kept growing and the sediments from the volcanic mountain ranges flowed into the ocean and slowly built up. The sea was growing ever shallower around the islands. By twelve million years ago there were two large passages: the more westerly one was in current-day Costa Rica, while the easterly one was in northern Colombia. There may have been lesser straits connecting the Pacific and Caribbean in Panama and Nicaragua.

The islands were really like icebergs, most of their bulk lying below water level. The chain of islands linked up underwater to form a vast sill that stopped the flow of deep-sea currents, long before surface waters were constricted or blocked. The great nineteenth-century American marine biologist, Alexander Agassiz, was the first to note that the deep-water creatures of the Caribbean were more closely related to those of the Pacific than the contiguous Atlantic. He even came to consider the Caribbean as a bay of the Pacific that had been cut off by the rise of the isthmus (a narrow strip of land connecting two relatively large land areas); and all this long before plate tectonics was even dreamed of!

The first effects of the forming isthmus were felt by the marine creatures of the depths. Deep-water sea urchins on either side of the isthmus are less closely related than their shallow-water relatives. Presumably this is because they have been isolated for longer.

Two very similar-looking deep-sea crustaceans live on either side of the present-day isthmus. They are known as a species pair, for they were once a single species. The deep water sill separated individuals that then evolved in isolation into new species. The phenomenon of species pairs seems most common in the crustacea, and some scientists have suggested that of the nearly 1,500 species of crabs found in Panama, nearly half are sister species. The process of creating species pairs has continued as the barrier has grown.

The green turtles that nested on beaches on either side of the islands became isolated from each other. Genetic studies have determined that even with the plethora of nesting beaches scattered around the tropical seas of the world, there are only two sub-species. One inhabits the Indo-Pacific, the other the Atlantic and Mediterranean and the split has been timed at approximately three million years ago. The turtles were not the only ocean-wanderers separated by the burgeoning barrier.

Humpback whales

Humpback whales have an interesting lifestyle. Their strategy is one of maximizing the input of food while minimizing danger, and this they do by utilizing their greatest asset – size. They are magnificent migrators. They spend the summer in the cold northern waters of the Atlantic and Pacific, where there is plentiful food. The long northern summer days and the rich nutrients of the seas bring a broth of plankton, clouding the water and providing sustenance for countless crustaceans and schools of silvery herring and capelin. These fish and shrimp lookalikes are the food of the humpback whales.

Humpback whales have many means of hunting their quarry, the most spectacular being bubble-netting. This technique is best used in the pursuit of fish shoals. The small pod of humpbacks dives deep, below the fish and, circling upwards, blows streams of bubbles. These create a wall of silver, enclosing the panicking fish, which swim towards the surface. To the excited observer on the surface, the first sign of the unfolding drama is the 'magical' appearance of a ring of bubbles on the surface. The next events are swift and awe-inspiring. Inside the enchanted ring, silvery fish explode out of the water. Thousands of herring, or capelin, skitter and dance over the surface in their panic and haste to escape. Then, as if in slow motion, the waters bulge and a huge black head and jaws appear. The humpback whales have swum vertically upwards under the fish, which, sensing the bow wave and their impending doom, swam for the surface. The whales, their heads still rising up out of the water, open their jaws, engulfing the fish. As the jaws close and the whales' huge heads sink back under the grey-green waters, so floods of water are forced out. The water is squeezed between the hairy plates of baleen that line the mouth, and the unfortunate fish are left inside the maws.

Fuelled by the fine feeding of the northern seas, the whales move south for the winter where conditions are very different. The warm blue waters, so apparently welcoming, are in fact a desert - there is little plankton to obscure the water. But the whales have not moved south to feed. The northern summer fare will sustain them through the tropical winter. The reason for the long migration south is most likely to do with reproduction. The males display and mate with the females in the winter, and the females give birth in the same season. The warm shallow waters are ideal for the babies. They may not be able to thermo-regulate efficiently, so the warmth is crucial for the first weeks of their life. Their mothers care for them, making sure they can reach the surface to breathe, and providing all the food they need as rich milk.

Up to three million years ago the two summer feeding groups, one from Newfoundland, Greenland and Iceland, the other from Alaska, met in the winter in the ancient tropical sea between the two American continents. Here males and females from both groups frolicked and mated. The volcanic chain of islands then lodged between the two continents and closed off the seaway. The two groups of humpback whales have been isolated breeding populations ever since. The Pacific humpbacks move across the vastness of that sea to the tiny mid-oceanic volcanic landmark of Hawaii, or swim south to Baja California. Their Atlantic relatives still travel down to winter near their old playgrounds. Today, they spend the colder months on the Silverbanks, north of the island of Hispaniola.

The stepping stones

The ever-growing volcanic islands formed stepping stones that stretched from South to North America. The slopes continued to shed their sediment into the seas. The silt built up and slowly constricted the flow of water between the islands until the surface waters were affected. The result was dramatic: the ocean currents, the great rivers of the sea, were redirected.

The westerly tropical flow across the Atlantic met an immovable object: the growing island barrier. The sea current was diverted northwards; the coriolis effect swirling the waters clockwise and along the coast of North America. The North Atlantic Drift and its small brother, the Gulf Stream, gained dramatically in strength. As the current is constricted between the Bahamas and the Florida coast, it flows at its fastest. If you stand on the beach of one of the Florida Keys and look out at the calm blue ocean, you can see a river in the sea. Weed, mangrove leaves, and sadly all too often today, plastic rubbish moves past at enormous speed. The effect is mesmeric and somewhat alarming. There is no obvious force, no powerful agency, just blue water and all its flotsam racing past. This is the Gulf Stream.

Further north, the diverted ocean current broadens and slows as it moves up past New England before continuing its clockwise rotation out into the northern Atlantic. Its final destination is the north European coast. The North Atlantic Drift is the bearer of the mild but damp English weather. The British Isles are spared the continental extremes of freezing winters and hot humid summers. The isles are at the same latitude as James Bay (the southern part of Hudson Bay), yet we do not see frozen oceans or polar bears. Instead, the west coast of Scotland boasts gardens with palm trees and other sub-tropical delights. The character of the British climate is, in a large part, written by the flowing hand of the North Atlantic Drift; and that came about because the gap between the American continents was blocked around three to four million years ago.

Ice-Age trigger?
There was a more extensive impact of the sea-current changes. The injection of a great body of warm water into the northern Atlantic changed the world climate (or at least contributed in a major way). The warm water increased the precipitation in northern latitudes. The increased cloud cover, and the areas of snow-covered ground, reflected more of the sun's heat. The ground cooled, more snow formed and more of the sun's energy was reflected back out into space. This positive feedback-loop helped bring on the global Ice Age, lowered sea levels and created the land connections between continents. In high latitudes, North America was reconnected with Asia. Large land mammals moved across in both directions. Mammoths and mastodons, giant bison and musk oxen moved into North America and were joined by deer and the wolf family. All these creatures were to play a part in the unfolding Central American drama. The change in the motion of the oceanic currents, and the lowered sea level due to the consequent Ice Age, had a profound effect on the life that inhabited the coasts of the tropical seaway.

Ridley turtle

The ever more substantial stepping stones affected another marine creature, the Ridley turtle. When this reptile species became trapped either side of the 'stepping stones' it evolved into two species: the olive Ridley and the Kemp's Ridley. The olive Ridley, which lives in the Pacific, has been a very successful species. On the third quarter of the moon, the sea off certain beaches takes on a strange appearance: thousands of turtles gather, the surface of the sea peppered by their heads as they take an infrequent breath. Staying just offshore for a few days, the number of turtles continues to grow, and males and females mate. Then, one night, they storm the beaches *en masse* with up to 100 000 females laying their eggs within the space of three frantic days and nights. Such is the pressure to breed, the contents of many earlier excavated nests are dug up by late-arriving females.

The olive Ridley's sister species is the Kemp's Ridley turtle. This eastern half of the clan is confined to the coastal waters of the Gulf of Mexico. There are no obvious differences in the behaviour or lifestyles of the two, yet Kemp's Ridley is an endangered species that never seems to have had the success of its western counterpart. In 1947, the turtles hauling ashore in Tamaulipas, Mexico, numbered approximately 40 000, but by 1978 there were less than 500 females on the beach. The Kemp's Ridley turtle is in serious trouble and the future is uncertain for this product of the formation of the land bridge.

The coatimundi is a relative of the first creatures that island-hopped south. It is an engaging rogue with a catholic diet that includes tarantulas and the eggs of the nesting turtles.

The amphibious island-hoppers

Even before the land bridge was complete there were creatures moving between the two continents. After eight million years how they actually made the transition is impossible to tell, but island-hopping by means of rafts or swimming may have played a large part. Ground sloths were a South American group of heavy-bodied herbivores and to them goes the honour of being the first mammals to cross the gap. They are, rather improbably, excellent swimmers and a powerful form of doggy paddle carried the first colonists north. They are known only from fossils – our prime source of evidence for the story of the land bridge – as are many of the other pioneers. The first known creature to move south was a member of the racoon family, the *Procyonids*. It was a larger creature than today's racoon or coatimundi, but shared their habits. It was almost certainly omnivorous and an opportunist, always sniffing out new food sources.

Why were the ground sloths and racoons the first 'heralds' of the subsequent invasions? Professor David Webb of the Florida State Museum, who has made a lifelong study of the interchange of animals across the land bridge, believes it is due to their lifestyles. Racoons are very curious carnivores, always exploring new places. They are also very good swimmers. The extinct ground sloths were generalist feeders, and so may have been a vegetarian equivalent of the racoon. The modern relatives of the ground sloths, creatures like the three-toed sloth are also excellent swimmers. So perhaps the mixture of a curious nature, combined with the ability to swim for long periods, gave these animals the edge. Whatever the truth, after these creatures swam across there was a hiatus of five million years before the great invasion started.

The improbable tree sloth has depended on the wetter climate and forests to make its slow progress along the land bridge. It is an excellent swimmer, like its ancient relatives the ground sloths.

When the land bridge was complete and mammals could move freely without 'getting their feet wet', there began one of the great events on earth. Rarely in the billions of years that life has existed on earth has such an opportunity occurred – two tribes of animals, from two continents, were about to meet. There had been minimal contact between the two groups for over 60 million years. Each was very different in character. What would happen when they met? This great experiment of nature is known in the scientific community as the Great American Interchange.

The Great American Interchange

The first mammals, for which we have evidence, to move south across the land bridge were not giant herbivores, or fierce predators, but field mice. Two million years ago, these small rodents were a great success in South America, and, in the period since their late Pliocene arrival, they have radiated out across the continent. There are now over 40 genera and hundreds of species. The field mice evolved and diversified to fill the great number of habitat types available in South America: from the high Andes to the lowland forests and deserts. Another northern group was a major success in South America. They had no competition, because, before cats and dogs headed down the isthmus of Panama, there were no true carnivores.

The first cat down was the 'sabre-toothed tiger', *Smilodon*, a fearsome predator that ambushed its large mammalian prey. The sabre-tooth was a very heavily built cat, with great muscular strength. The sheer bulk of such cats precluded them running any distance. The physique necessary to grapple with large mammals was opposed to the thin, long limbs required for sustained running. Large carnivores must either ambush large prey or run down smaller victims. The muscular sabre-tooth must have leapt out from the cover of the undergrowth, sprinted the short distance to its intended victim, and leapt on to the back of the hapless mammal. The cat's sabre teeth were designed to slash and rip at the throat of the surprised victim, and the subsequent puncturing of windpipe and neck arteries would have led to a rapid weakening and a swift death. Sabre-tooth tigers disappeared from both North and South America when large 'antiquated' herbivores, such as the ground sloths, became extinct.

The jaguar, a peerless predator, is also an expert proponent of the ambush. Less specialized in its eating habits than the sabre-tooth, it preys on anything from turkeys to tapirs, with white-tailed deer and peccaries among its most frequent prey. It moved down the forests that have intermittently clothed the land bridge over the last two million years. With its pelt spotted and blotched as disguise, it is a forest cat. In the rainforest there is as much activity at night as during the day, and the jaguar has highly sensitive eyes for hunting in the nocturnal gloom. The back of the eye has a reflective layer called the *tapetum*. This acts like a mirror, bouncing light that has passed straight through the layer of receptors, the retina. In this manner, the cat almost doubles the sensitivity of its eyes. Whenever anyone confronts its eyeshine in the depths of the night-dark forest, there is an instant prickle of fear and awe. The jaguar, one of a small band of Central American creatures that demand respect, is a very impressive animal.

It was not alone on its journey south – the smaller cats, such as the ocelot and the marguay, also moved down through the wooded terrain. Before the closure of the land bridge, South America had no cats; afterwards, it had more species than anywhere else on earth. The same holds true of the canids, the wild dogs. One of these, the wolf, with its long thin legs and stamina to run down its prey, has the opposite hunting strategy to the jaguar. Unlike the solitary jaguar, it hunts in packs over open ground. The only thing it has in common with the top cat of Central America is its success and its ability to hunt large mammals. The dogs would have travelled down the land bridge during one of the drier glacial periods when the ground-cover was predominantly grass.

The *Procyonids* had a second invasion of the south. The living *Procyonids*, the racoons, coatimundis, kinkajous and ringtails almost certainly evolved in Central America. There is only one genus found in South America that is not in Central America, so the group seems to have evolved and diversified in the tropics just north of the land bridge before spreading south. These adaptable omnivores have also moved north, and, in the case of the racoon, even claimed Canadian city suburbs as their own.

Several other important groups of mammals raced, pottered or dawdled down the land bridge. Among the more notable were the bears, tapirs and the horses. The horses became extinct in both continents, but not before some had moved into Asia via the Bering land bridge. As will be seen in a later chapter, it was the Spaniards who brought the horse back to its evolutionary home. The camels fared slightly better. The North American camels marched into South America during one of the cool grassland periods, only for their North American ancestors to go extinct. So, today, this bizarre family has a very curious distribution with one branch of the family in Asia and Africa, and the Andean tribe of llamas, vicuñas and alpacas in South America.

The squirrels moved down through the forests into South America, crossing over with the monkeys that moved north. Both groups are wholly dependent on trees for food, shelter and highways. The squirrels have a varied diet based around nuts, while the monkeys feed mostly on fruit and leaves. The squirrels' range spread through Central America and down as far as the tropical forests of coastal Brazil, which, today, are under so much threat. Monkeys were confined to Central America, reaching as far north as southern Mexico. They are a tropical group, and their current limits seem to be defined by the tropical forest. The squirrels, which were originally a temperate group, have fared better in the sub-tropical regions of their southern homeland. The monkeys, though, were among the last of the southern invaders.

What of the other creatures that moved north? The ground sloths moved up the land bridge at an early date, and were already buried and on the way to immortality as a Californian fossil 2.5 million years ago. These were relatives of the sloths that beat the 'traffic jam' and swam north over five million years earlier. Further 'toothless wonders', and also relatives of the sloths, were the glyptodonts. These were tank-like creatures that looked like armadillos. They had a tough flexible shell as a defence, backed up by a club-like tail. Like their relatives the ground sloths, the glyptodonts went extinct along with most of the large grazing mammals.

A surviving group of North American mammals that originated in the southern continent are the porcupines. The most common porcupine is a tough customer, and not just in terms of its spiny defence. Porcupines range all the way north to Canada; and you are just as likely to see a porcupine stroll nonchalantly across a road in the spruce forests of coastal Alaska, as to see them in the wooded mountains of Central America.

The anteaters moved north about two million years ago. There are fossils of giant anteaters that are nearly two million years old in northern Mexico. Today no anteaters are found further north than Central America.

The great majority of the animals that took part in the great adventure of the American Interchange were creatures of open country. Particularly in the first million years, from 2.5 to 1.5 million years ago, large herbivores like horses and camels, glyptodonts and ground sloths dominated the scene. The reason lies with the Ice Age. The cooler drier conditions led to savannah-type habitats. These grasslands acted as filters, allowing the large herbivores safe passage while blocking the movement of creatures of the woods. Only in the last half-million years have forests come to dominate the isthmus. They now extend from northern Colombia to Costa Rica. The forests have provided an aerial highway along which the squirrels and kinkajous of the north have journeyed – crossing over with the monkeys, tree sloths and possums from the south.

The opossums are a very South American family. They are marsupials, part of the Gondwana heritage that South America shares with Australia. This was among the last groups to move into North America, arriving about one million years ago. North America still has its curious opossum, a large rat-like creature, which carries its youngsters strung out along its bald tail. But Central America has much greater riches. There is even an aquatic marsupial called the yapok. It has partially

The armadillo is a modern, distant relative of the giant glyptodont.
It has been a successful traveller from the south.

webbed feet, and, more curious still, its pouch faces backwards, so that it does not fill with water and create drag when the yapok is swimming. The yapok is a great aquatic hunter in the streams of Central America.

What about the fish?

Fish seem a very odd group to look at while talking about a dry land-bridge connection, but, surprisingly, they help tell the story. As we read earlier about the fishes in the Greater Antilles, there are two types of freshwater fishes: those that live only in fresh water, the primary freshwater fishes, and those that can swim in and out of brackish water, unsurprisingly called the secondary freshwater fishes.

On the Caribbean islands there are no primary freshwater fishes, which suggests there were never dry-land connections to the continents, or, if there were, they were 'fleeting' in duration. What about the land bridge, a solid volcanic gang-plank between two continents, that is full of freshwater fishes? How have these migrated on to the isthmus?

The secondary freshwater fishes have been enormously successful in Central America. Just as in the Caribbean, they have managed to move across the shallow waters, lagoons and brackish waters between the volcanic islands. They were almost certainly the first to lay claim to the rivers flowing down from the volcanic highlands into the Pacific and Caribbean. The cichlids, a large and very successful group of fishes, moved up the island margins from South America. Having evolved in western Gondwana, they are naturally found in both Africa and South America. They are hardy and aggressive fish that vigorously defend their territories. This gives them a great advantage over other colonizers.

Cichlids also have a wonderful and varied set of reproductive behaviours. Typically, a small number of eggs is laid on a meticulously cleaned rock or leaf. One or both of the parents then guards the eggs from the numerous potential predators. At its simplest, the male or female may hover attentively over the eggs. The parent's wafting fins fan the eggs with a stream of water that keeps the eggs aerated. But some cichlids go further, and take up the fertilized eggs into their mouths where they are brooded. Here, there is even greater safety and a guaranteed flow of oxygen-rich water. This mouth-brooding may be performed by either male or female fish, depending on the particular species. Many fishes are fine examples of sexual equality when it comes to raising a family. The cichlids display very sophisticated behaviour compared to other fishes. In particular, the aggressive defence of territory and elaborate parental care have been major advantages in their spread into Central America. Cichlids are still rapidly evolving in the region, creating many new species, and an equal number of headaches for taxonomists trying to understand what is going on.

The solid connection of North and South America has allowed primary freshwater fish to migrate on to both continents. No North American fish have made it further south than Lake Nicaragua, which is strictly north of the land bridge. Characinae are a huge family of ancient African–South American origin. The most famous characin is the much-feared, much-hyped piranha. Less well known relatives have successfully navigated up the land bridge. One genera, *Astyanax*, a true pioneering spirit, has made it as far north as the Rio Grande of Texas.

How can fish move across land? The answer is they don't – except, that is, for eels and the magnificent 'walking catfish' that can actively propel themselves over wet ground, at least for short distances. In this curious awkward manner, these fish can travel from one pond or river to another. To traverse the dry land bridge, the small delicate fish, with gills that would suffocate in air, stayed firmly in their aquatic environment until, on a grand timescale, the changing landscape became their means of travel.

The land bridge in particular is a very active landscape. Volcanoes erupt and then erode, earthquakes remodel the land. These processes take place over hundreds of thousands of years. The rivers are forced to change course, and, as they do, they take their fishes with them. So the many rivers, running roughly parallel, have often merged their waters as lava flows and earthquakes force their courses together. Erosion may also remove barriers between the tributary streams, mingling their waters. In this manner, fish slowly move up and down the land bridge. Huge floods, which might only come about every thousand years, may create temporary sheets of water linking several rivers.

The Ice Age fluctuations would have had an influence, too. The rising and falling sea levels uncovered and then inundated the coastal lowlands. When the sea level was low, several separate, but neighbouring, rivers may have come together on the exposed plains, their water mingling and flowing into a larger river. As the sea level rose again, the rivers once more took on their individual identities, the sea covering up the evidence of the freshwater connection. The fishes, though, would have mingled and would now be in all the rivers. Freshwater fishes move with their rivers.

The climatic gateway

The Ice Age sea-level changes that exposed and flooded the coastal aprons of flat land were a part of the same climatic changes that switched the isthmus gateway from mist-shrouded tropical forests to open-wooded grasslands. The spine of the isthmus, the highlands, has always sucked up the moisture of the clouds that glide in from the Atlantic. At the peak of the Ice Age it may have been open oak and pine woodland. Today, it is one of the wettest places on earth. The trees drip with moisture and support veritable gardens of mosses, ferns, bromeliads and orchids. A large tree may support many tonnes of rotting and living vegetation. This is the home of the resplendent quetzal, a bird that can claim to be the most beautiful on earth. The quetzal is an aberrant trogon. Trogons are rather dour insect-eaters, which tend to spend a large part of the day sitting upright in the lower branches of a tree. Despite being gaudily coloured, with bright plumage, they are hard to spot because patches of colour break up the outline of the bird among the tangle of twigs and leaves, shadow and dappled light. Trogons are found in South America, Africa and Asia. They are probably birds of Gondwanaland. The ancestors of the quetzal most likely travelled up the land bridge, and stayed and evolved in the cloud forests into one of the wonders of the natural world. The resplendent quetzal has relatives in the highland forests to the south, but none compares in magnificence.

Quetzals are never more beautiful than at the beginning of the breeding season. Freshly plumed, the males, in a mantle of glittering golden green, their 'false' tail

The cloud forest is one of the glories of Central America. In this cool cloud-wrapped world,
trees are festooned with ferns and bromeliads. This is the home of the resplendent quetzal.

feathers stretched out to twice the length of the red-bellied body, show off their
outrageous beauty to its best, performing courtship flights, their gorgeous train of
feathers trailing and undulating behind their bicolour bodies. Several males may try to
win a female. They dig false nest holes and the female selects the best of the beautiful
bunch and settles down to serious nest-building. The chicks are born in April or May
just before the arrival of the rainy season. The quetzal has a specialized diet, its primary
source of food being the fruits of a myrtle tree, a kind of wild avocado. Before you
have visions of the quetzal trying to swallow an avocado fruit whole, I should say that
this wild relative is much smaller – more the size of an olive. The quetzal has formed a
partnership with the 'wild avocado'. It plucks the fruits from the tree while on the

wing. This seems to be relictual behaviour from the birds' insect-catching ancestors. The avocado obligingly places its fruit out on the furthest twigs, which helps its preferred partner the quetzal, but deters other less welcome fruit-eaters. The bargain between bird and tree is simple, the quetzal gets its meal and the tree spreads its seeds.

Dispersal of plants

Paradoxical as it seems, plants are far better travellers than animals. While the great majority of the land mammals had to wait for the completion of the land bridge, many plants had crossed from continent to continent much earlier. With the exception of a very few, plants don't move. They depend on their seeds – designed to be transported by agents as different as the wind, sea, birds, mammals and reptiles – to transport the next generation.

The temperate trees of North America moved, by way of their mobile gametes, along the mountain tops of Central America. These volcanic way-stations were cool and wet, and the trees – oaks, firs, pines, elms, poplars (cottonwoods), and walnuts – were ideally suited to the climate of these islands in the sky. These familiar trees migrated down into South America, along the rising spine of the Andes. Some, like *Juglans*, the walnut, arrived in the highlands of Ecuador, 20 million years ago. Others like the oaks and alders, a few hundred thousand years ago. The trees were not alone as they travelled south to claim the cool highlands. They were accompanied by members of many familiar, northern-hemisphere, temperate plant families: buttercups, poppies, primulas, roses, violas, heathers, clematis, violets, and even nettles 'hopped' along the island mountain tops.

Having evolved on an isolated continent that had long had a temperate climate, the plants of the North American Continent were ideally suited to the fingers of high ground that ran north-south. The lowlands that lay between the volcanic highlands came to be dominated by the plants of South America. That continent had evolved a huge array of tropical species, particularly in the Amazon basin. These plants could now move up into the tropical lowlands of Central America. Most would not move further north, because, with the increasing latitude, the climate was cooler. The Ice Ages acted like an opening and closing gate. During this time, the lowlands appear to have been drier, and grasslands predominated, allowing many of the great herbivores to trundle down the land bridge. When there was a warm interlude, and the sea level rose, the narrowed land bridge was blanketed in the exuberant green of tropical rainforest, and the monkeys and sloths could now move north.

In the drier periods, the lowland lying between the mountains and the Pacific would have been extremely arid. The rain-clouds came, as they do today, from the east. The high mountains stole all the moisture from the clouds and the cool currents of the Pacific kept the air dry. This long sliver of land would have been a desert. Members of the cactus family must have migrated north along this intermittent channel. The giant saguaro, sentinel of many a 'Western movie', entered North America by this route. It has a close relative that lives in the arid Monte region of Argentina. These giant spiky cousins are separated today by thousands of kilometres of mountain and rainforest, but, at one time, there may have been slivers of desert that stretched out across the continents, from Arizona to Argentina.

The consequences of the connection

The formation of the land bridge was the last of the great earth-moving events that shaped Central America and the Caribbean. Over vast spans of time, these geological occurrences had a profound effect on the life of the region. The Greater Antillean islands had 'cruised' into the Caribbean with their own passenger list, including frogs and todies. The Lesser Antilles, smaller and newer, had to depend on misfortune for their pioneers. Hurricanes and Orinoco floods brought parrots and anole lizards. The Caribbean islands are defined by few but very distinct species of animals, and a distinct lack of mammals. The mammals of two continents met and mixed on the land bridge that formed from the next wave of Pacific volcanic islands. Some, like camels and porcupines, moved on into the heart of a new continent; many stayed to populate Central America. The tropical forests filled with monkeys from the south and killer-cats, such as the jaguar, from the north.

There was just one piece of the jigsaw, one final jewel in the extraordinary panoply of plants and animals that makes the region the richest on earth. That was people – *Homo sapiens* – the last to arrive, but destined to have the greatest impact of all.

Part II

THE PEOPLE

CHAPTER 6

FROM FIRST
ARRIVALS TO
FIRST CIVILIZATION

The last piece to be added to the complex jigsaw that is Central America and the Caribbean was our own species, humans. They arrived from the north, that much is certain, but thereafter much is conjecture and dispute. The closing of the land bridge between North and South America changed the pattern of oceanic currents. This may have initiated a cooling of the climate on a global scale, with the Ice Age opening up the Americas to the first wave of humans. The cold meant that, over the northerly latitudes, water fell as snow rather than rain. The snow stayed on the ground and, slowly, layer on layer accumulated. The snow's own weight then compressed it into ice. Over hundreds of years the compacted ice became a deeper and deeper blue as a great thickness built up.

The Ice Age was marked by vast continental ice sheets that crept south over North America, Europe and Siberia. These sheets were thousands of metres thick in places, and locked away much of the water that otherwise resided in the oceans. At the height of the Ice Age, 18 000 years ago, the ice sheets had a volume of 77 million cubic kilometres. As a result, the sea level plummeted as much as 100 metres, exposing a large amount of land that had been shallow sea floor. The lowered sea level would have created a 'land bridge' connecting Siberia with Alaska. This was very different in character to the volcanic, mountainous and tropical isthmus that linked the two American continents. Beringia is the name applied to the land connecting eastern Asia to the far north-west of North America. Now covered by the grey turbulent waters of the Bering Sea, 14 000 years ago it would have been a windswept treeless plain. Beringia stretched over 1000 kilometres between the continents and hundreds of kilometres north to south. The vegetation was ground-hugging tundra shrubs and grasses – a vast bleak prairie studded with lakes. During the Ice Age, the climate would have been very inhospitable.

So why did humans move out on to this lost land of Beringia? The answer lies with the two things that favoured Beringia. It was ice-free, while most of the northern latitudes of Asia and America were submerged under layers of frozen water. Equally important, Beringia had the grasses to support herds of giant grazers, such as mammoth and bison. These attractions drew hunters into Alaska. There was no flag-planting ceremony because these nomadic hunters could not have known they had moved into a new world, and would never have known they were the first humans to walk on American soil. They were just going about their nomadic business of following the herds of four-legged food. Despite the fact that the first

PREVIOUS PAGES: A terracotta jaguar from the sixth-century Zapotec culture of Mexico.
The Zapotecs were among the first cultures with writing and the ceremonial calendar.
The jaguar has a man inside its mouth, and around its face are cobs of corn.
Fear of, and spiritual reverence for, the predator, and the dependence on maize
are all represented in this powerful work of art.

Americans are unknown to us, or even to themselves, this was a momentous event. Two continents, upon which had evolved a huge and rich array of life forms in complete isolation from human beings, had been invaded by the most destructive of species – humans. The continents would never be the same again.

We cannot really say with any great certainty when people first arrived. The Ice Age was not a simple lowering of the sea level, followed by the big melt and the 'tide coming in'. There were many fluctuations in the temperature, and the size of the Beringia land bridge varied accordingly. Scientists, interested in the origins of early man, have argued that the oscillating sea levels created windows of opportunity when the first nomadic hunters could have crossed. There was such an opening around 25 000 years ago, then a watery impediment to travel until approximately 14 000 to 12 000 years ago. After that, the sea levels rose decisively to drown Beringia 10 000 years ago. The evidence from archaeological sites is not clear cut, but favours the arrival of humans in North America around 13 000 years ago.

All this assumes that the early hunters could not have paddled their own canoe, but there is no reason to assume there were no sea-crafts. However incongruous it is to picture the hunters of mammoths carrying canoes, it is possible that they travelled by sea in simple craft without sails. They would not have been open-ocean voyagers, but would have hugged the coastline. If this scenario has any validity, then Beringia, in one of many of its shrinking and expanding guises, would have had to exist. It is hard to imagine people paddling in an open craft across the width of the Bering Sea. To this day, it is a formidable body of icy cold water, often fog-bound, subject to violent storms, and frozen over for part of the year. Even the modern Innuit or Eskimo, excellent sailors, are known to have crossed only at the narrowest point, the Bering Straight, which is a distance of 80 kilometres. For these reasons, the evidence points to people arriving in Alaska, by an overland route, at least 13 000 years ago, but maybe earlier.

Early hunters: 13 000–7000 BC

There were narrow north-south 'corridors' of land between the ice fields that still stretched across most of the continent. These must have been the routes taken by the nomadic hunters and gatherers. The strips of ice-free terrain would have been similar in appearance to Beringia, though with a scattering of hardy trees, such as spruce. The animals would have been similar, too: bison, mammoths and giant sloths, relatives of today's ponderous denizen of the Central American rainforest canopy. These sloths were purely terrestrial though, and they were huge. There were also horses, not to be ridden, but hunted for food.

PRE-COLUMBIAN SETTLEMENTS

The bands of hunters moved quickly to spread out over the grassy plains south of the ice fields. If the later date of arrival, approximately 13 000 years ago, is correct, then humans populated the virgin paradise of the Americas in just a few thousand years. There is evidence of hunting parties in Patagonia, dating back 9000 years.

These earliest hunters are often portrayed in the action of ambushing or running down large spectacular herbivores, but they also caught small rodents, even mice. In fact, these smaller mammals and birds were more important as food than the mammoths. Most important of all, and least glamorous, was the gathering of wild fruits, seeds and nuts. These mis-named 'big game' hunters arrived in present-day Mexico before 9000 BC. The climate, then, was very different. Today, much of inland Mexico is arid and semi-arid, with deserts stretching south from the border with the USA to the Valley of Mexico. Then it would have been much wetter. The influence of the waning Ice Age would still have been considerable. Where today there is a harsh sun glaring down on a dry dusty landscape, 10 000 years ago there were clouds, heavy and grey with rain, sweeping up the mountains and on to the plateau. The temperature was cooler. The landscape would have been verdant with tall grasses, punctuated by oak and pine trees. Most surprising of all, the Valley of Mexico would have been almost filled by a huge shallow lake teeming with fish and fowl. It would have been a great place to be a 'hunter-gatherer'.

I have already said that the small nomadic bands depended more on rodents and snakes than mighty mammoths, but how did these people, with only the most simple of weapons, stone-pointed spears and stone axes, hunt such huge powerful animals? The real power in their limited arsenal was the *atatl*, a notched throwing stick. The rear-end of a spear was placed in the groove of the *atatl*, the butt tucked against a peg. The *atatl* and spear were then held horizontally, at head height. The spear was launched from the *atatl* with the same action as throwing a ball. The *atatl* acted as an extension to the hunter's arm, increasing the speed of the spear and the distance it could travel. A spear propelled in this way has been scientifically shown to have 200 times the impact of a hand-thrown one. This was the technology with which they faced the fearsome thick-skinned mammoth.

Big-game hunting

Mammoth-hunting must have been a team activity. A small band of men (presumably a male activity, like hunting in most other cultures) would have ambushed or run down the giant beast. In the Valley of Mexico, remains of mammoths have been unearthed that suggest a scenario of hunting that involved great courage and skill.

The imperial mammoth, a colossus, standing four metres tall, appeared to favour the swampy reedy fringes of the lake, spending its days uprooting and feasting on the lush vegetation. In the early morning or late evening, the hunters, their presence veiled by the deceptive half-light, would have crept up on the beast, cutting off its escape towards dry land. The men would have constantly checked the fickle breezes to ensure that a change in wind-direction did not carry their scent to the mammoth and give them away. The beast would then have been charged and attacked with *atatl*-launched spears. A team-leader would have been essential to co-ordinate the hunt because the hunters would have had to get within throwing distance and attack at the same time. As many spears as possible would have had to pierce the huge side of the mammoth, and the men would have doubtless shouted and screamed as they ran towards the beast to frighten the wounded mammoth into running away from them. If they did not, there would have been a danger of them being charged by an irate mammoth, and in the marshy terrain there was little chance of them hiding or outrunning the angry curved-tusked Goliath.

In a successful first attack, the mammoth would be panicked into charging away from the hunters and into the lake. The lake was very shallow, but it was underlain by a deep layer of sticky mud. The heavy leviathan sank up to its belly in the ooze. Once ensnared, the hunters would have moved in for the kill. Even now there was great danger. The huge animal was difficult to kill. The men had to approach the thrashing bellowing beast and drive a spear into its lungs or belly. This could only be done at close quarters, within the reach of grasping trunk and puncturing tusks. The rewards were a huge surfeit of fresh meat, and great prestige for the hunters. The successful completion of a hunt must have been marked by feasting and festivities.

Disappearance of the big-game animals

The great fertility of Central America at the end of the Ice Age was brought about by the wet climate. By 7000 years ago, the climate had swung the other way. Instead of being wetter and cooler than today, the world's climate became hotter. In Central America, the grasslands became deserts and scrub, and the numerous lakes shrank. The days of the 'big-game' hunting were coming to an end. The megafauna, as it is known, became extinct about this time. It is still argued whether it was the change in climate, and the loss of the vast grasslands, or over-hunting by the first Americans, that caused the extermination of the giant bison, the mammoths, and the giant ground sloths. Perhaps it was both: a mixture of hunting pressure and loss of habitat. Either way, the world lost some of the most spectacular mammals at a time when small mobile bands of people were hunting them.

The hunting groups had to adapt to the dryer, meaner conditions. They lived alongside the ever-decreasing lakes, where there were still waterfowl to be hunted and fishes to be caught. They were likely to have been migratory people, who spent the winters and summers in different locations, always drawn to where food could be gathered or hunted. Collecting wild seeds must have become an ever more important activity as the climate continued to deteriorate and protein became scarcer and harder to obtain. The seeds of wild plants were gathered and prepared for consumption by grinding and boiling into a gruel.

Today, there are still a few elderly Native Americans who gather wild seeds and nuts: in the Great Basin Desert of western USA small groups of women of the Ute tribe spend the late summer among the pine and oak groves of the mountain slopes. The climate and vegetation is very similar to how it would have been 7000 years ago in Mexico. The sky is crystal blue, the air dry and full of the scent of pines and aromatic herbs. Pine cones are collected, and kernels shaken free to be tossed and roasted on a woven sheet over an open fire. Acorns are gathered and ground into a flour, which is then soaked to remove the tannins – chemicals in the acorn that are bitter and toxic and there to deter seed-predators from destroying the oak's investment in future generations. Once the tannin has leached out into the water, the poisonous fluid is poured off, and the acorn mush is heated by dropping hot stones into it. The result is a nutty-flavoured porridge.

The hunting and gathering way of life sustained the early people of Mexico for many generations, but a great change was taking place. The ancient hunters and gatherers already had the technology for food-processing, and when they achieved the domestication of maize, they started a revolution that led to the great civilizations of Central America.

Change to agriculture

These early people, shadows to us 5000 years later, were able to make one of the greatest transitions in the history of humankind. The wealth of resources of upland areas of Central Mexico allowed the hunter-gatherer bands to settle for long periods. There were lakes on which to fish and hunt wildfowl, and wooded slopes where turkeys could be trapped, and fruit and nuts harvested. The richness that allowed semi-permanent settlements opened new horizons. They began to experiment with the genetics of other life forms, or, more prosaically, they became farmers.

How did these people move from a life of gathering wild food to becoming harvesters of crops? In the case of maize, the argument goes something like this: the gatherers would have selectively collected the bigger seed heads of a wild grass, inadvertently scattering them while the seeds were being processed for eating. Some of the seed would have germinated around the camp, and, at some point, this accidental genetic interference would have been formalized by intentionally planting the bigger kernels of the wild ancestor of what was to become maize. When they started to clear the land of weeds in readiness for the seeds, then farming began. The seeds were most likely popped into holes made by a sharpened planting stick, still a common agricultural implement in Mexico.

From Mexico, the maize revolution spread to the north and south, allowing nomadic hunters to settle and settled hunters to expand their populations. But that is another story, first the story of maize.

In the early 1960s an archaeologist from the USA, Dr Richard MacNeish, was investigating some dry caves in the Tehuacán Valley, 200 kilometres to the south-east of Mexico City. While probing gently into the dusty cave-floor, he discovered some small seed heads. They were only five centimetres long and bore eight rows of six to nine seeds. The significance of these miniature corn-on-the-cobs far outweighs their size, for they are among the earliest evidence of farming and true agriculture. These tiny cobs were not wild, they had been engineered by human hand, planted and harvested. The most recent dating techniques give the cobs the grand old age of 4700 years.

How did ancestral corn turn into maize? There is great controversy about this crucial issue, fuelled in part by the gaps in our understanding. Two theories dominate. In the first, maize is believed to have evolved from an unknown wild

ABOVE: A wild male turkey. The turkey was long hunted in Mexico
before it was domesticated by native peoples.

OPPOSITE: The many modern forms of maize reflect the thousands of years
of domestication in the Americas.

plant. The closest candidate is a strange variety of maize, a genetic aberration, called pod corn. Unlike the modern plant, pod-corn kernels (seeds) are enclosed in a skin or chaff and the head of corn is not fully covered by husks. The importance of that is that the primitive pod corn, unlike maize, could disperse its seed without human help. It is only partially domesticated. In this scenario, the hypothetical wild ancestral corn is conceived as having only one female flower on top of the single stalk, and just below the male tassel. The female flower turns into the seed head or cob after fertilization. The cob would have been small with all the features of pod corn. The only problem is no one has ever found such a wild ancestor.

The actual transformation of pod corn into maize is still the subject of lively debate, but a consensus may be appearing. It is thought that pod corn was crossed with perennial *teosinte*, a wild grass and close relative, to produce the ancestral form of maize. The hybrid that resulted had many features of a domesticated crop. The amount of chaff or 'waste' around the kernels was reduced, and there were more and bigger kernels. The husks completely covered the head or cob, so that the seeds could no longer be dispersed naturally. Equally important, while the male flower or tassel remained atop the plant, several female flowers developed lower down, so more cobs could be carried by the one plant. The plant was being genetically manipulated to increase its yield.

The second theory has the advantage that it has a candidate wild ancestor. *Teosinte* fulfils this role. In fact, there are six species of *teosinte*, three annual and three perennial, and genetics has confirmed that one annual type is very closely related to maize. The problem with this theory is that no *teosinte* has been found in cave sites associated with humans, and, moreover, modern Mexicans find the plant distasteful. So, one theory has archaeological evidence and a process of domestication, but no ancestor; the other has genetics on its side and an ancestor, but no process of domestication and no archaeological evidence. Perhaps there is some middle ground?

The plant with which the early Mexican farmers experimented – and which was found in the caves of Tehuacán – is a kind of popcorn. It has many wild features apart from its small size and number of seeds. It sits somewhere between pod corn and modern maize, and could have reverted back to a wild plant. In truth, the cave-finds can be fitted into either theory. What is needed is further fieldwork to find older, more primitive domesticated maize, along with a plant-breeding programme to replicate the hypothetical harnessing of *teosinte*.

The effects of the domestication of maize on the people were profound. In the Valley of Tehuacán, small hamlets of five to ten houses appeared around 3000 BC. Permanent settlements were now possible, and, with growing permanence, came possessions, such as pottery, that were too cumbersome and fragile for people with a migratory lifestyle. The first crude ceramic wares appeared around 2000 BC. Alongside maize, the all-important staple, these sedentary people farmed beans, squash, pumpkins and chile peppers – crops which may have been domesticated at around the same time as maize. In the centuries before the great civilizations of Central America emerged, however, wild plants and animals continued to supply the majority of the calories for the first farmers.

The beginnings of civilization

This huge span of time, called the Preclassic, 1800 BC–AD 150, saw the consolidation of farming, and the development of permanent settlements into villages. Why did it take so long for village life to take shape after the domestication of maize? Part of the answer may lie in the domestication, a process that is still not fully understood. The size of the cob and the number of kernels may have increased with repeated back-crossing with the wild relative, *teosinte*. There was most likely a long period when maize was not productive enough to support settlements larger than hamlets, never mind the arts and crafts of larger village life. Some scientists suspect that the increase in yield from maize occurred suddenly, as a result of further hybridization, and the appearance of pottery, weaving and sacred works of art around 1800 BC is a direct result of this agricultural event.

It is an aside, but the long delay between the start of the domestication of maize and the first towns left American civilizations lagging behind those of the Near East that were based on cultivated wheat. From those early farmers came the European civilizations that were to voyage to the Americas with catastrophic consequences for the Mexican civilizations. Had maize proven to be more amenable to domestication, and had cities grown up earlier in Central America, it might have been the Aztecs who set sail for Southern Europe, rather than the reverse. An intriguing if wholly hypothetical aside.

There was another factor that might have contributed to the delay in the appearance of village life – the climate. Throughout the period of the domestication of maize, the climate was dry. By 1800 BC, it had turned wet again. The rains would have certainly increased the productivity of the land, which may have supported more people. Whatever the reason, the appearance of the village marks the beginning of the civilizations of Central America. (Archaeologists talk, more correctly, of the meso-American civilizations, as the Valley of Mexico is strictly outside Central America. But to keep the number of geographical terms to a minimum, we will continue to talk of Central America, allowing it to expand to take in Central Mexico.) The villages in the Valley of Oaxaca grew in size from ten or less houses, about fifty persons, to over ten times that size in the first 500 years of settled farming.

Maize, as ever, was the staple, but avocados were cultivated, along with chilies and squashes. The villagers still hunted deer and peccary, and ate domesticated turkeys and dogs (this latter food source may sound bizarre, and disgusting to us in our pet-oriented culture, but it is little different to our domestication of pigs for the pot).

The villages in the Valley of Oaxaca give us our first glimpse of the specializations and hierarchies that mark advanced societies. Archaeologists have found that certain houses appeared to concentrate on certain crafts. One such craft was the making of mirrors from magnetite, a kind of iron ore. The magnetite is laboriously polished until it takes on a highly burnished reflective surface. The burials of these early agricultural people are the strongest evidence of a social hierarchy. The number of goods – magnetite mirrors, pottery, and jade carvings – placed with the body shows some members of the village to have had high social status.

The maize revolution was happening, in parallel, in several places in Mexico. In the Valley of Mexico itself, archaeologists have uncovered a lakeside village that

The Oaxaca Valley, the site of one of the earliest civilizations. The domestication of maize allowed the growth of permanent townships, and the creation of social hierarchies and artisans.

supported a rich aristocratic class. Their burials include many ceramic figurines. Most are of naked women, which may be fertility figures, but there is also a male figure that is thought to be a ball-player. The ball game, played by two teams with protective coverings for hands, knees and hips, is a characteristic and distinctive feature of Central American cultures. The Maya and Aztec, the later best-known civilizations, both played the ball game, as did the Taino people of the Caribbean. The game is thought to be about divination, a means of resolving which of the complementary but opposite forces of the supernatural – the productive, fruitful, and the destructive, chaotic – will succeed in the future. The two teams represent the two kinds of forces that control people's lives. The figure of a ball-player, dating from about 1300 BC, is the first hard evidence of a ceremonial game that became an important element in Central American civilizations.

The inexorable growth of villages into towns, and family bands into hierarchical societies, is clearly seen in the development of temples. At their simplest, these are thatched buildings like an everyday house, but elevated on an earthen platform. The platform could then be increased in size, and faced with stone. The stone could be covered in a smooth finish of stucco, the platforms growing, one atop another. At Cuicuilco, just to the south of the present-day 'megalopolis' of Mexico City, there is a large early example of temple-building. The platform is faced with stone and rises in four tiers to twenty metres. It is an imposing structure, for it is over 100 metres in diameter, and the labourers would have had to carry many thousands of tonnes of rubble to build such a mound. The population size of this local town is estimated to have been around 20 000. The site was abandoned when a volcano erupted and lava-flows covered the town and the temple platform. But before the unknown folk of the Valley of Mexico fled from the violence of the volcanic eruptions, the first civilization in Central America had blossomed in the humid lowlands of the Gulf of Mexico.

The Olmecs
These people created the most ancient civilization of Central America. Where they came from, what they called themselves and what language they spoke, are all unknown. Their name is borrowed. 'Olmeca' were the 'rubber people', described by the Aztecs to the early Spanish chroniclers as living in the steamy swampy jungles of the Gulf coast. This area is not immediately welcoming. The climate is very hot and humid and the land low-lying and swampy. It must have been an unhealthy place, and a difficult one to move around in, for there are a myriad winding waterways, all slowly emptying into the Gulf. So why was this the location of the first flowering of civilization? There are almost certainly a number of reasons, but, paradoxically, two might be the climate and the swamps.

The Gulf coast receives both summer and winter rains. The Olmecs could have easily produced two crops of maize a year from the rich alluvial soils. The slow-flowing rivers were teeming with fish, which seem to have constituted the most important source of protein, though the ubiquitous dog was also considered food.

The Olmec civilization, based on the fertility of the land, produced some of the most powerful works of art in the Americas. For the most part, these represent gods and spirits, and elements in their mythical stories. The carvings are striking not just because of the quality of the work, but also the subjects. The most famous are the were-jaguars. These are figures that appear to be half-jaguar, half-human. It is argued that Olmec mythology is based on a mother goddess sleeping with a jaguar and producing these strange childlike creatures with fangs. The Olmec took other creatures into their pantheon of gods. There are caiman and harpy eagles, both animals of their lowland jungle home. The shark is also depicted in their sacred art. All these animals are fearsome predators, creatures that still strike awe and respect (and a little fear?) in the minds of modern folk.

The jaguar kills the same creatures that the Olmec people hunted, but with greater ease. It hunts largely at night while men roam the forest during the day. The jaguar was not only respected for its predatory prowess, it was feared for its ability to overpower and kill a man as easily as a deer. Many cultures, such as the later Maya and Aztec, related the jaguar's fierceness to warriorhood, and this may have been the case for the Olmec, too. The jaguar is a creature of the spirit world, one associated with the shaman, the healer and communicator with that world. The jaguar can see in the night, into the realm of the spirits and dreams.

Like many pre-scientific cultures, the Olmec seem to have credited animals with souls. The creatures could come to them in dreams, as could people. There were no solid bodies in either case, just the spirits of the animal or person. So there was an equality at the spirit level between the natural world of plants and animals and humans. It is little wonder that they could accept that, in mythical times, a goddess and jaguar had sex and produced were-jaguars. Disconcerting creatures for us to look upon, the were-jaguars combine the cuddliness of plump-bodied babies with the snarling face of a jaguar. The top of the head is always cleft. Why? After 3000 years it would be hard for anyone to answer that; but this has not stopped people speculating. Might it be a congenital defect, such as spina bifida? Were these were-jaguars deformed children? Were they sacrificed as monsters? Or is the cleft the result of a sacrificial blow by an axe? We do not know, but, despite our modern comforts and the huge gulf of time and understanding that separates us from their Olmec creators, the figures have the power to disturb us.

Recently, there has been another theory put forward to explain these disconcerting figurines: the cleft head, thick lips and general plumpness could mean that they are modelled on toads. Or they may be composite creatures, made of elements of toad, jaguar and human. Why a toad? In the lush lowlands where the Olmec lived there is a large amphibian called the marine toad. It has parietal glands behind the eye that are full of toxins, and these toxins are known to be psychotropic and produce a changed state of awareness. There are people today who 'get high' licking these toads. Could it be that the toads were revered because they allowed the Olmec to escape the 'normal', to communicate with the spirit world? Large numbers of toad bones were found in the same area where the dog and fish bones were unearthed. Unlike the fish and domesticated dogs, it is unlikely that the Olmec were eating the toads, so were they keeping them for ceremonial use?

Toads and frogs are important animals throughout Central America and its many cultures. Their status comes from their unusual characteristics. They live in two worlds, those of water and land, which makes them special. They are associated with fertility, both because they lay large numbers of eggs, and because they call and mate at the time the rains bring back fertility to the soil and crops. (The marine toad is an exception here because it breeds in the winter, but then in the Olmec lowlands there

ABOVE: An Olmec were-jaguar. Is it part jaguar or part toad? Its strange appearance matches the features of the marine toad (OPPOSITE), but we may never know. The figure still retains the power to disturb.

is no sharp distinction between the wet and dry seasons.) Finally toads and frogs 'magically' transform themselves from tadpoles. These powers make them as fascinating to us today as they must have been to a people just as intelligent and curious as us but without any scientific understanding of nature and life. Were-jaguar or fierce transformer toad, the fact that both hypotheses are tenable warns of the difficulties in trying to understand a lost people through their few remnants – a problem faced again when looking at the Taino in chapter 8. The characteristic of the creatures that most impressed the Olmecs is fierceness. Their deities are mostly based on jaguars, sharks, harpy and caiman eagles – all very powerful predators.

War and destruction

The Olmec civilization was based on agricultural territory, and they seemed quite capable of waging war over it. From the sudden violent destruction of Olmec settlements, to the macabre find of butchered burnt human bones that suggest cannibalism, there is evidence of war. When the Olmec towns were excavated colossal heads were discovered. These are most impressive, imposing works of art, thought to represent the chiefs of the Olmec towns. Frequently found badly damaged, it is probable that the conquering forces smashed and defaced these monuments to vanquished rulers. They were not only defaced but ritually buried, as if locking away any spiritual power the huge carved heads might retain. It has been argued that war became frequent when agriculture produced settlements and arable land. There was now something to fight over – the rich land that the townships were based upon. Whether this is true, or too much of a simplification, warfare is evident among the settlements of the earliest civilization.

Land may not have been the only thing they fought over. Trade routes would have become important for the artisan and élite classes, as they gathered precious and sacred objects. These objects must have held great fascination and a kind of magic. The substance, magnetite or jade, was beautiful in its own right, and the craftsmanship created an object with great power. There would have been the same curious combination of reverence and avarice attached to these supreme works of art as today can be seen in the collecting of impressionist paintings. The reverence would have helped increase their value as religious objects and the avarice may have led to battles over ownership of the objects, the trade routes and the mineral sources.

The trade routes were a source of wealth to another new specialized group – the traders. The Olmec traders brought in magnetite rocks to make mirrors, or as finished artefacts. They also traded for jade and obsidian. Many of the minerals they required were from the highlands. Some, such as obsidian, volcanic glass, were the products of the violent birth of the region. The Olmecs established trade routes and possibly satellite townships along the routes, establishing a style that would remain a characteristic of subsequent Central American civilizations. In two other important instances, the Olmecs are the originators of key elements of later civilizations.

First calendar

The Olmecs had a calendar. A curious one to our eyes, it was to become universal in Central America, and continued in use in rural Maya areas until very recently. The calendar consisted of 13 numbered months, each of 20 named days. The 260-day year started with one caiman. The calendar appears to have been largely ritual in function, for rulers and gods are often named by their 'birthday'. The calendar was also used to help track celestial events, such as the movement of constellations, and the eclipses of sun and moon. The development of a calendar points to the increasing importance and power of rulers who could stamp their authority on the society through naming themselves and their gods after calendric days.

The 260-day ritual calendar was not the only one. There was also a solar calendar composed of 18 months of 20 days, with a short period of five days to make up the numbers. In the same way as the ritual calendar, each day of the year had a unique combination of number and name. The calendars set out together with one caiman, but obviously quickly diverged and the sacred period of 52 years is required for the calendars to mesh once more. Cycles of this duration were fundamental to later Central American civilizations.

First writing

Glyphs, carved symbols, appear first at Monte Albán in the Valley of Oaxaca. This is the homeland of the Zapotec, another early warlike civilization that shared many features with the Olmecs, including ritual killing and mutilation of enemy rulers, and the ceremonial calendar. These earliest examples of writing seem to be dedicated to recording the dates of conquests over neighbouring city 'states'. Glyphs, however, soon appear, in a more sophisticated manner, in other Central American cultures, the most famous of which is the Maya.

Chapter 7

Mysteries

of the Maya

The Maya lowlands, from whence sprang the greatest culture of the Americas, are not an obvious cradle of civilization. They are covered in monsoon forests that grow out of a limestone platform, riddled with caves and sink-holes. In places, the limestone comes to the surface, elsewhere there is a thin layer of poor soil, while in some of the river valleys and depressions there are peaty swamps. The forests are full of fearful beasts, from poisonous snakes and jaguars, to myriad disease-carrying mosquitoes. For seven months of the year, from May to November, there is rain, but the remaining period is one of drought. The land that stretches from Honduras up into the provinces of Chiapas and the Yucatán of Mexico is a tough place to scrape a living, never mind construct a huge civilization, yet the Maya did just that. There are many mysteries associated with the Maya, one of the greatest being: why did great and magnificent cities spring up in the midst of a tropical forest?

All cities need feeding and, even here, there is a Maya mystery, for some scholars have calculated that the land could not have produced enough food to support the population. The traditional method of farming in the tropics is to 'slash and burn'. The trees are cut or ring-barked to kill them, and the scrub, understorey and trees are then burnt. The ground is cleared to let in sunlight, and, at the same time, the soil is fertilized by the ash of the burnt vegetation. Tropical soils are notoriously poor because all the nutrients are locked up in the trees. The leaves and branches that fall to the forest floor are quickly rotted and recycled by fungus. Very little goodness ever reaches the soil, which, for hundreds or thousands of years, has had the minerals leached from it.

So 'slash and burn' is admirably suited to the tropical forests of the Maya lowlands. The only problem is that, within a few years, the soil loses its ash-borne fertility and reverts to its original exhausted state. When that happens the *milpa*, the small field, must be given up to the forest and a new patch cut and burned. So the Maya farmers would have had to move their maize fields every three or so years, leaving the land to slowly revert to forest. It may have been as much as ten years before another crop could be grown. The result was that only a minority of the land could have been worked at any one time, but the Maya population is estimated to have been many millions. How did it feed itself?

In recent years, as scientists started to ask how the citizens were supported, some exciting discoveries have been made. The answer appears to be that the Maya were more sophisticated farmers than we had given them credit for. The steep hillside slopes had very thin soil, which held very little moisture, and were

PREVIOUS PAGES: The jaguar, powerful predator of the Maya lowlands,
spirit-animal and god of the underworld of night.

susceptible to erosion, so the Maya terraced them to overcome these limitations. The soil then built up behind the rubble walls, held more moisture, was richer, and so produced a higher yield of food plants. Down in the swampy valleys, the Maya farmers faced the opposite problems and had to find a way of draining the land. Ditches were dug, criss-crossing the swamps. The soil from the canals was heaped up on to the tiny plots, giving greater drainage and deep fertile soils. The canals lowered the water levels and provided access to the small plots. Every time the waterways were cleared more rich smelly ooze was deposited on the raised fields. The Maya use of raised fields predates the similar Aztec *chinampas* system (see chapter 9) by a thousand years.

The Maya even had a solution for dry lowland plains – irrigation. Over a period of 300 years, the Maya of Edzná, a coastal city, and the most impressive irrigation site, built a canal to connect their town to a local river. But this was no ordinary canal. It was 11 kilometres long and up to 100 metres wide, all dug by hand using Stone Age tools. The Maya not only brought water to the city, but built reservoirs to store the precious fluid. Professor Ray Matheny, who led the archaeological team, has calculated that the irrigation system could store 2700 million litres of water. The only statistic more stupendous than that is the effort expended: 1.68 million man-days of back-breaking physical labour. These very sophisticated farming practices allowed the Maya population to expand to a size ten times greater than could have been supported by 'slash and burn' alone. But, having said that, the farmer was not wholly responsible for the growth in population.

The Maya civilization was based on maize, the staple of all the great ancient cultures of Central America. Maize, although a good staple food, is not perfect in dietary terms. It lacks both niacin, which is one of many Vitamin Bs, and several amino acids, the building blocks of proteins. The Maya solution was to boil up the maize kernels (not the soft sweet seeds of sweetcorn, but bullet-hard maize) with lime. The one thing there was no shortage of was lime. The chemistry of the cooking pot released niacin and adjusted the balance of amino acids. Without the *mixtamal* process, the Maya would have suffered from malnutrition. Along with the increasing yield from maize as ever more domestication took place, the *mixtamal* cooking process must have played a part in increasing population numbers.

Central America is one of the richest places on earth for bees – or, more accurately, for *Hymenoptera*, the family to which bees belong. There are many kinds of bees and wasps, some of alarming size and appearance. The one bee that is not naturally present is the honey-bee. It has been introduced, of course, as elsewhere in the world (and now is causing problems as the racial hybrid 'killer-

Maya Settlements

bee'). The absence of the honey-bee was of no import to the Maya for they had already 'domesticated' the stingless bee. Maya farmers in the Yucatán still keep stingless bees. The technique is to offer the bees a place to build a nest in hollowed-out sections of log with just a small entrance hole at one end and sealed up with mud at the other end. When the farmer wishes to collect honey, he simply opens up one end, takes some honeycomb, and then reseals the entrance. Honey met the needs of the Maya sweet tooth, but what of the need for protein?

The Maya appear to have kept specially bred maize-fed dogs for food. Did this habit come from the more ancient culture of the Olmecs who, as we read in the previous chapter, also dined on dogs? Perhaps. Another Maya source of protein – turkey – is more to our taste. Turkeys are natural wild inhabitants of Central and North America. The Maya farmer did, and still does, rear turkeys. It was from Central and North America that the Spaniards brought the bird back to Europe. Although the domesticated dog and turkey supplied much of the meat in the Maya diet, they still hunted wild animals – deer and peccary being the most important species of the chase. Other wild foods included a range of fruit trees.

There is some debate as to whether the Maya had gardens of preferred fruiting trees. Certainly, in some patches of the forest, there appears to be an unnatural abundance of useful trees, such as sapodilla and breadnut. Some have argued that the ancient Maya would have weeded out the unwanted saplings to encourage the growth of more useful food trees – thus producing a giant

The white-tailed deer: shy forest denizen and the prey of jaguar and the Maya.

rainforest orchard. This may or may not prove to be the case, but papaya, avocado and custard apple, a delicious fruit with a creamy pulp and large hard seeds that catch out the unwary, were certainly on the Maya menu.

Cacao was a great luxury and very valuable crop. The beans, flavoured with various spices including chili, were made into a drink only for the élite, and traded, almost as currency, with the civilizations to the north in the Mexico highlands. The small trees, which needed shade from larger trees or bushes, grew only in well-watered moist soil. The Maya heartland, with its porous limestone and dry season, was not the place for cacao, the most important growing area was the Pacific slope of the southern highlands. It may have been the major economic crop of that region and the most important item of trade.

Limestone was the bedrock of Maya civilization. Except for the volcanic highlands in the far south (where most cacao was grown), all Maya settlements were on a great shelf of limestone that juts north into the Caribbean. There were few rivers or surface water, for the limestone was permeated with caverns and caves. Water that fell as rain simply disappeared underground to percolate through the interstices of the rock, appearing at the surface only as pockets of swamp. Rains in the Maya lowlands had the same seasonal cycle as elsewhere in Central

America. The heaviest downpours were from May to December, with a dry season for the remaining four months. This was a real problem for any form of permanent settlement. Where was water to be found? Initially it appears that villages were set up beside *cenotes*. *Cenote* is a Spanish derivation of the Maya *dzonot*, water-filled circular holes in the limestone. They are formed when the roof of a cave collapses, and some of them are of considerable size and depth. The *cenote*, which is replenished from underground streams and rivers that meander through the limestone, is a permanent supply of water and played an important role in Maya religion and ceremony.

The irrigation systems, noted above, were certainly not just for agriculture – they must have also helped to overcome the lack of drinking water. The northern region of the peninsula had the lowest and least reliable rainfall. There are low hills here which have the benefit of rich soils, but these were settled late because of the lack of water. Even subterranean water was hundreds of feet down. The solution was to dig storage pits into the rock. These underground tanks, called *chultunob*, were bottle-shaped and surrounding the entrance was a gently sloping, smoothly plastered area of ground that directed the rainwater into the cistern. The basic elements of water, rock and food were the foundations on which the Maya civilization was constructed.

The Preclassic period

The Maya were remarkably slow off the starting blocks. While the Olmec were already highly sophisticated, and other civilizations were flourishing in the Mexican highlands to the north, the Maya lowlands appear to have been a backwater. The area was very densely settled by 1000 BC, but there was no sign of advanced civilization. Cuello, a small site in northern Belize, has been thoroughly excavated by the archaeologist, Norman Hammond, and his discoveries have pushed back the start of Maya civilization by several hundreds of years. Maize husks from the site suggest that the size of the maize cob had been steadily increasing; and that, from 1000 BC to AD 200, maize yields doubled. This, combined with *mixtamal* food-processing, would have allowed the population to increase dramatically. A large efficient agricultural population, able to support an élite, is a basic prerequisite for the growth of civilization.

Cuello has other intriguing discoveries. There were pieces of jade placed in some of the burials that Professor Hammond's team excavated. These burials were not equally well endowed with precious objects, such as jade and pottery, and this may reflect a class-based society, with an élite, and perhaps even a ruler. Tantalizing fragments of stone hinted that the citizens of this small town practised writing and were numerate. There was a temple platform constructed of limestone blocks. The temple was only small, the platform four metres high, but the find could represent the beginning of a process that would lead to the great temples of Tikal. What was the impetus that moved the Maya from densely populated villages to the stage, marked by Cuello, where religion, writing, and arts seem to be combined with the first hint of a stratified society? Jade may be a part of the answer. Sources of precious jade are very rare, and the people who coveted it may have brought their cultural influence.

The Olmec civilization flourished from 1400 BC, and certainly had writing, a calendar, and an elaborate religion. Their cities were ruled by an élite who held great power and demanded precious objects, such as jade. There is little evidence to suggest that the Olmec traded generally with the Maya. For the most part there would be no reason for the Olmec to do so, for the Maya were relatively backward and had little that the Olmec wanted – except, that is, jade.

Some of the most extraordinary Olmec art is executed on jade celts (axe heads). They were probably made of jade because this was the hardest substance known to the people of Central America and could keep an edge. As such, it would have been ideally suited for axe heads. Its durability must have imbued it with the precious power of permanence and the thought that jade might last for eternity may also have made it important as a gift to the gods. It may have been by this line of logic that celts came to be carved with were-jaguars by the Olmecs. Whatever the logic, the Olmecs traded for jade, and the best source was the Motagua River in present-day Guatemala. Rounded river-washed boulders of the mineral jadeite were collected from the banks and stream bed, and the Olmec traders, or their middlemen, brought not just exotic items for barter but the influence of their culture to the Maya cities near the precious jade source. The Maya probably acquired their reverence for jade from the Olmec. The colour green was precious: it was maize, water, and the startling, iridescent, false tail-feathers of the quetzal. The Olmecs greatest influence, however, was the means of keeping track of time and the seasons, and the great art of writing.

Calendar Round

All civilizations need a way of marking the passage of time and the civilizations of Central America used a system called the Calendar Round. The Maya most likely learned the means of recording time from the Olmecs. The Calendar Round is a most unusual system. It is really two cycles, one of 260 days and one of 365. The latter is obviously a rough approximation of the annual solar cycle that we call the year. But what was the 260 cycle all about? We do not know; it is so unusual that it remains one of the great conundrums of American civilization. Whatever the logic of its origins the 260-day cycle was used to mark ceremonial and ritual

events and, for that reason, is sometimes called the Almanac Year. The 365-day cycle is known as the Vague Year, as it is six hours short of the true length of the solar year.

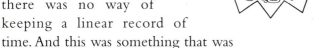

The problem with the two calendars of the Calendar Round is that they were so cyclical that there was no way of keeping a linear record of time. And this was something that was becoming important to the rulers, as they traced their alleged ancestry back to the distant past. How could they do this if there was no way of recording time past the last cycle of 52 years? It was as if the original Calendar Round had been enough to map out an individual's lifetime, but as Maya society, and in particular its rulers, outgrew it, they needed something more sophisticated, something able to record a dynasty. The answer the Maya came up with was the Long Count, and the start of the Classic period is defined by the use of this calendar. It is not, however, Maya by invention – again the Olmecs may have introduced this means of tracking huge periods of time, but the Maya developed the Long Count to its greatest glory.

The Long Count

The Long Count is really quite separate from the Calendar Round. It is based on a set of nested periods starting with 20 days.

20 kins	1 uinal	20 days
18 uinals	1 tun	360 days
20 tuns	1 katun	7200 days
20 katuns	1 baktun	144 000 days

ABOVE: The complex intermeshing of the Almanac (left) and Vague Years (right). The counting system is based on dots and bars, and allows 13- and 20-day months for the two calendars. The month glyphs and names are depicted on the respective 'cogs'.

OPPOSITE: Tikal today, set in the rainforest of Guatemala. It would have been more magnificent in its heyday, with plastered and painted exteriors.

With this system, the Maya were now able to plot huge cycles of time, lasting 13 baktuns or over 5000 years. The Long Count starts from the day the universe was created, or re-created. For the Maya, the present universe began on the equivalent of 13 August 3111 BC and so will end on 23 of December 2012.

The great Preclassic cities

While the Calendar Round was present, evidence of the Long Count and the use of writing is sparse in the Preclassic period. Yet Maya architecture was already advanced at the end of this 2000-year period. In cities, such as El Mirador, Nabke, Uaxactún and Tikal, large platform and temple complexes were constructed. The Maya lowlands were 'blessed' with unlimited building materials. Limestone was carved into blocks with chert tools – no mean feat, but easier than one might imagine, as the limestone is relatively soft. It forms its hard outer skin only after it has been exposed to the elements. The limestone could also be burnt to form lime. When this was mixed with water, the result was a tough durable plaster which gave the Maya architect great scope to use his creativity.

Stepped temples and their bases rose to a height of 70 metres above the surrounding country in cities such as El Mirador. The temples were made of a façade of limestone blocks with a massive rubble infill. These stone-clad 'mountains' were impressive enough, but around 300 BC the Maya began to enhance the impact of these extraordinary structures, covering the stone façade with plaster. At most sites this stucco was so deep that it could be carved. The final touch was that of a brush, as the stucco was painted. These must have looked astonishing when they were new.

At Nabke, Dr Richard Hansen has uncovered the largest known Maya architectural carving: a mask of Vucub Caquix, an early deity. The mask is over ten metres long and nearly five metres high. Dr Hansen has an interesting theory about the Maya who built these impressive cities and temples. As we have seen, there are few Long Counts or examples of writing in the Preclassic period but Dr Hansen also noted that the artwork was largely about the gods and that the temples were dedicated to the deities. There are no royal tombs, no records of the ruler's great works, no great dynastic chronologies. Could it be that, in this early period, the cult of the ruler had yet to be established? The élite, who had the temples erected, may have had leaders who led a privileged life with special access to the gods, but the leaders may not have been hereditary leaders, or seen themselves as semi-divine – as descended from gods in distant mythical times. All that was to follow in the Classic period.

The Classic period

In the period AD 250-900, the Maya reached intellectual heights no other pre-Columbian culture in the New World would ever match.

Tikal, in the Guatemala lowlands, was one of the earliest and largest Classic Maya sites. It had continued to grow from an impressive Preclassic city, and excavations have revealed a settlement at the site from 600 BC. Today, Tikal is a splendid site, with lowering temples in the rain-soaked mist-shrouded forests. It feels more like a Hollywood set than an ancient ruined city. At its peak Tikal must have been a truly magnificent sight. Temple IV, its top 70 metres high, reached up over the forest canopy. The city and 'suburbs' covered 64 square kilometres, there were 3000 buildings and a population of 40 000 people. Yet the streets were not planned or formally laid out and there were no defensive walls. This huge city needed food and water. The forest for many kilometres all around must have been felled very early on to provide farmland. It has been calculated that the citizens of Tikal consumed 131 tonnes of salt a year. (The salt was produced on the north coast of Yucatán in lagoons that are still operated today.) There were ten reservoirs for water storage to supply the populace through the dry season from December to May. (It is still so tough to survive in Tikal that one reservoir had to be refurbished to supply drinking water for the archaeologists who spent 15 years excavating the site in the 1950s and 1960s.)

The rulers of Maya cities set out to increase their own status in the eyes of their citizens. Early rulers of cities, such as Nabke, had aligned themselves with the gods, and so enhanced their prestige. The artwork and monuments were dedicated to the ancestor gods. The rulers of Tikal appear to have taken the same route as those of Nabke, and now erected memorial stones or stelae commemorating their own actions during their reigns, and those of their nearest relatives. These stelae have allowed the deciphering of the Maya written language. Some of the earliest, from the third century AD, tell of warfare between cities but it may turn out to be more accurate to describe it as ritualized battles between the rulers. The purpose seems to have been the taking of prisoners rather than conquest, and the captives were sacrificed at important events of commemoration.

Warfare and sacrifice

The Maya had foot soldiers (there were no large domesticated animals in Central America), whose role was to infiltrate a neighbouring, hostile city's territory and to capture, *not* kill, prisoners. The soldiers wore tunics made of tapir hide, which would have provided some protection from *atatl*-propelled spears. The hostilities were typically ambushes, and the success was measured by the status of the captives taken.

ABOVE: A detail from the Bonampak murals, showing the jaguar-skin-clad élite with their hapless captives. The victims were gruesomely tortured.

LEFT: Baird's tapir, in its favourite haunt, a forest stream. The tapir was hunted by the Maya for its meat. The animal's tough thick hide was used by warriors for protection from enemy spears.

The murals at the city of Bonampak tell the story of a war in the late Classic period, around AD 790. There is a series of paintings, laid out like the most beautifully executed cartoon. The early scenes are of the ambush and battle in the forest, then, in wondrous detail and glorious colour, the murals reveal the fate of the captives. The location is presumably the royal palace or one of the stepped temples in Bonampak, and the prisoners are wearing only loin cloths in contrast to the victorious ruler and his élite who wear jaguar skins, and fabulous headdresses. One of the fallen soldiers is kneeling before the ruler, Chaan-muan, presumably pleading for his life. The captives are obviously being tortured, some graphically spurting blood from their fingertips, the nails having been torn, one by one, from their fingers. A head lies on a bed of leaves, the body nowhere to be seen – decapitation was the typical form of execution of prisoners.

The next scenes, showing pictures of dancing, celebrations and blood-letting, give some clues as to why the Bonampak élite had waged such a strange and, to our eyes, barbaric war. The battle was to capture prisoners in order to torture and behead them as part of the ceremonies and celebrations to commemorate a new heir to the throne of Bonampak.

Why, in general, did the Maya wage such bizarre warfare? Might it have been to increase the status of the rulers over their neighbours? As the rulers came to see themselves as divine, so they had more to prove about their powers to their own people. What better way to show their superiority than to defeat the powers of the nearby competing divine rulers. The humiliation of torture and execution may have emphasized to the populace of the conquering ruler the worthlessness of other deities? Could this curious style of ritualized warfare be the reason why cities were not defended by walls and ramparts? All is speculation. We may never know the motives of the rulers, but we have learned of their names and their lineages through the deciphering of the Maya script.

Mayan writing
Until recently, Maya hieroglyphics remained a puzzle. The few signs that had been deciphered related to dates in the calendar, numbers, and astronomical events, and the remaining symbols were thought to refer to similar arcane subjects. As these appeared to be the only things the Maya wrote about, they were held to be an intellectual race of star-gazers, obsessed by patterns in time and space that they could track in the night sky. The Maya cities were without walls, and so the Maya were considered rather other-worldly and peaceful, and the cities to be really ceremonial centres. This view was most eloquently expressed by the great Maya scholar, Sir Eric Thompson:

The great theme of Maya civilization is the passage of time — the wide concept of the mystery of eternity and the narrower concept of the divisions of time into their equivalents of centuries, years, months and days. The rhythm of time enchanted the Maya; the never-ending flow of days from the eternity of the future into the eternity of the past filled them with wonder.

But then two people — one a Russian linguist, Yuri Knorosov, who had previously worked on Egyptian hieroglyphs, the other an artist and archaeologist, Tatiana Proskouriakoff — made dramatic linguistic breakthroughs that changed our opinions of the Maya. Yuri Knorosov's great discovery was that the script was not purely ideographic, with each symbol representing a concept, but rather there were also glyphs for syllables, sounds and for specific meanings. The script combined the two types of symbol to increase its readability and interpretability.

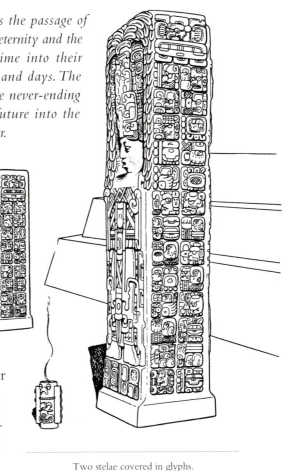

Two stelae covered in glyphs.

It is an irony that this device of the Maya kept their writing undeciphered for so long. It was a fate of history that, after the first early attempts at translation based on phonetics had failed, later scholars held the script to be ideographic. The cracking of the signs for the calendar and astronomical events just reinforced this interpretation. Knorosov saw that there were not enough glyphs to express the number of concepts or ideas required for a complex society, and too many for them to stand for sounds. The script, therefore, must be a hybrid combining both elements. Knorosov published his findings in the 1950s, but his work was not widely accepted for over 20 years. There was the wisdom of the learned and eloquent Thompson in opposition. Furthermore, the period was the height of the Cold War, and Knorosov was not only a Soviet but one with strong Marxist tendencies. His cause was helped in the 1960s by Tatiana Proskouriakoff, an American who was born in Siberia.

A gifted artist and archaeologist, Tatiana Proskouriakoff worked in the Carnegie Institute examining the glyphs from the Maya city of Piedras Negras. She realized that the stelae, the carved stone pillars in front of the temples and the plazas, were not randomly spaced, but occurred in groups. When she looked at the glyphs on these groups of stelae, some signs kept reappearing. The dates, one of the few glyphs that were understood, referred to periods of fifty or so years. Proskouriakoff's great intuition was that these hitherto indecipherable glyphs were markers of an individual's lifetime. The signs that kept reappearing were those for birth, accession to the throne, marriage, conquest in war, birth of children and death. Soon it was realized that there were other glyphs for battles and ritual blood-letting, and for relatives of the ruler. The writing was not an esoteric technical notation for star-gazers, but a history of the rulers. It was a means of recording their deeds, and of enhancing their repute, by connecting them back to esteemed ancestors, and back further to gods in the mythical past, now made concrete by the Long Count calendar.

The influence of Teotihuacán

Maya warfare was largely about increasing the status of one city's élite at the expense of another's. But there were 'real' wars where rulers expanded their territory and even captured other cities. How common territorial warfare was is still uncertain. What is known, courtesy of the dynastic stelae, is that Great-Jaguar-Paw, the ninth ruler of Tikal, changed the rules of warfare in his area. Great-Jaguar-Paw's brother, Smoking-Frog, captured the neighbouring rival city of Uaxactún. The date is recorded as 16 January 378. What was different was that Smoking-Frog not only dispatched the ruler of Uaxactún, he took over the city and ruled it himself. There is evidence that suggests that Smoking-Frog also sacrificed the whole royal line, women and children, to guarantee the end of the competing dynasty. Why had warfare escalated? The influence of Teotihuacán is suspected. This was the great civilization of Central Mexico. The metropolis was the largest city ever constructed in pre-Columbian America. It grew to be the sixth largest city in the world in the sixth century. The society was undoubtedly very warlike. Excavations have revealed mass sacrifices of young men, probably warriors. Some scholars hold that there were warrior and trader classes.

Teotihuacán had been trading with the two rival cities of Tikal and Uaxactún for over a hundred years before Smoking-Frog's celebrated conquest.

Lady Xoc in front of her husband, Shield-Jaguar. She is pulling a rope of thorns through her tongue, part of a sacred ceremony to communicate with the gods.

Had the rivalry for the privilege to trade with Teotihuacán caused the change in warfare? Had Smoking-Frog and Great-Jaguar-Paw escalated the stakes? It would seem so. But Teotihuacán's warlike influence appears to have come directly into play, for Smoking-Frog is depicted in clothes and holding weapons that are in the very distinct style of Teotihuacán. Over the decades of trade links, the militaristic style of Teotihuacán had gained sway in the Maya forests.

In the early years of the fifth century, the grandson of Great-Jaguar-Paw, Stormy Sky, became ruler of Tikal. Stormy Sky erected monuments to his own honour during his reign. One shows him with two figures dressed as Teotihuacán warriors on either side. The hieroglyphs make clear that, in fact, the two figures are of the one person, Stormy Sky's father, Curl-Nose. What does this mean? It is hard to say, for it could be anything from a Teotihuacán élite ruling Tikal to the local rulers taking on the warrior mantle of Teotihuacán to increase their prestige. Whatever the answer, prestige was all-important to the Maya rulers of the Classic period. The rule of Tikal was assured and the power of the city state would continue to grow for another 500 years.

The greatest of the rulers of Tikal was Ah Cacaw. He came to the throne in AD 682. Ah Cacaw commissioned two huge temples in his lifetime. Temple I was to be his burial place, where he lay undisturbed until 1961 when archaeologists discovered him deep inside the 40-metre structure. The transformation of rulers, from earthly leaders with privileged access to the gods, to deities in their own right, seems complete with Ah Cacaw and the later rulers of Tikal. Ah Cacaw had his own likeness carved huge upon the ornate roof 'comb' atop Temple I. This was a temple dedicated to the ruler who was a deity, not to any ancient gods.

Mystic blood-letting

Among the most stupendous of all Maya carvings are those of Lady Xoc, the wife of the ruler of the city of Yaxchilán. His name is Shield-Jaguar, and in one carving he is standing over Lady Xoc while she pulls a rope of thorns through her tongue. If one is feeling sympathy pains for Lady Xoc, and wondering why the ruler Shield-Jaguar is not grating a hole in his tongue, the reason is that his blood-letting is even more excruciatingly awful. The instrument used was a stingray spine, and the blood issued forth from the king's penis. Why would the élite perform such painful rites?

Scholars believe that the custom of blood-letting was a form of communication with the gods. The rulers, divine descendants, may well have entered into a trance-like state caused by the loss of blood, and in this changed state of awareness the ruler and his relatives may have entered the world of the gods. We may call it hallucinations, but for Maya kings and queens the rite of blood-letting and the subsequent communication with the spirit world was real and very important. Another carving shows a Vision Serpent, which denotes the line of communication or sight with the underworld of spirits, Xibalbá. It was here that important gods of the Maya pantheon lived, as well as the ancestors of the rulers. The Jaguar of the Underworld, the form of the sun as it travelled through Xibalbá during the hours of darkness, resided here. The rulers had to communicate with the gods to discover the current and future state of the universe. It was a form of divination, the rulers interceded for their people to discover if good or ill fortune was their lot.

But why the massive loss of blood? There were other means of hallucinating. One of the more unusual was the use of enemas when a rubber bag was filled with either alcohol, or a juice made from the highly psychotropic peyote cactus, and administered by way of a bone tube. The results would have mirrored blood-letting, without the pain. Perhaps the letting of blood was important in itself. The Maya believed that the people of the current world were fashioned by the gods from their own blood mixed with maize meal. By shedding their own blood the divine rulers may have been repaying the debt to the gods.

Whatever the truth, the scene must have been awe-inspiring. On important days, calculated using the Almanac calendar, the ruler and some of the élite, possibly relatives, would climb the long flight of steep steps and enter one of the narrow rooms atop the temple. Here they would release the flow of precious blood and enter into the world of Xibalbá. The ruler then returned to this world. He would appear from the gloom of the narrow room on to the temple platform, and, lit by flickering torches and starlight, stand in full view of the populace of the city, his clothes splattered in royal blood.

Professor David Stuart has found evidence in the hieroglyphic writings that the spilt blood was collected on paper, and the blood-soaked paper set alight. The clouds of smoke invoked the gods to send clouds of rain. Whatever the nature of the ceremony or its exact meaning, the letting of blood by the rulers was a way of keeping order in a universe constantly under threat of chaos. Cosmic balance between the spirit and earthly worlds was precarious. People had to repay the gods for their gifts of rain, sunshine, and fertility. This they achieved by means of respect shown by the numerous ceremonies and sacrifices. The divine ruler was the centre of these ceremonies.

The Maya universe

This was made up of the 13 layers of heaven, the earth and the nine layers of the underworld, Xibalbá. The sun, moon and planets, which moved against the background of the stars, were considered to be celestial beings or deities. They

ABOVE: The ball court at Copán is the best preserved of the many examples in Maya cities. The macaw-head markers can just be made out along the sloping sides.

OPPOSITE: A statue of a ball player wearing a skull headdress. The non-recreational nature of the 'game' is clear from this fearsome figure.

travelled below the horizon each night, through the layered underworld, to reappear at dawn. The green ceiba tree was conceived as the centre of the universe, the *axis mundi*. Its roots went down to the underworld, its branches stretched up to the heavens. The earth was flat and four-cornered. It was seen as the back of a monstrous crocodile that sat in a pool of water lilies. (Were the water lilies seen as stars? Had the Maya noted that they open and close their stellar-shaped flowers at dawn and dusk?) The ability to track the celestial bodies allowed the Maya élite to predict important events, such as eclipses, that caused anxiety, and also to plan the great round of rituals that was elaborated in the 260-day year. All events, be they impending warfare or births, could be considered in the light of the night sky. What did the celestial deities reveal? Was this an auspicious time to fight, would the newly-born ruler have a life full of fortune?

The ball game is one of the most distinctive elements of Central American culture. Yet though it appears ubiquitous, we do not really understand how it was played, or the rules or their significance. However, scholars have managed to pull together enough scattered evidence to paint a picture that is both intriguing and terrible. The game was probably played with slightly different variations at the many ball courts in the Maya cities. Copán, the finest ball court remaining, has sloping sides and carved macaw heads as markers for the game. The rules must almost certainly have changed over the hundreds of years that the game was played. Paintings on pieces of pottery depict two teams of men in protective clothing hitting a ball to each other. The ball was made of solid rubber and must have been both heavy and hard. The general object of the game seems to have been to keep the ball off the ground and to pass it back to the opposing team using the sloping walls of the court. Any part of the body, except the hands and feet, were allowed to contact the ball. The game in several guises is still played today in Central America.

The game was not a recreational sport. The stakes were very high. The outcome of the game was seen as an omen as to the future behaviour of the cosmos. The two teams symbolized the forces of the universe, and the ruler looked upon it as a form of divination. The teams may have represented different aspects of the deities: the sway of Xibalbá over the heavens, the Jaguar of the Underworld as opposed to the Sun God. The losing team often paid for their failure with their lives – sacrificed as repayment to the gods. The odds may often have been stacked in favour of one side, for captives are known to have formed one side. They lost and were sacrificed and the divine ruler of the city had the desired omens. There is even evidence that captive rulers or nobles of other cities were bound and used as the ball, until the rough-and-tumble of the game killed them. We do not know whether the ball game gave any sign of the collapse of the Maya civilization, but collapse it suddenly did, and just when it appeared to be at its zenith.

The collapse of the Maya

The heir to Bonampak, in whose honour the murals were painted and captives tortured and beheaded, probably never ascended to his hereditary throne. Bonampak was abandoned before the sequence of murals was completed. It was, however, not only small cities such as Bonampak that tumbled, the giant metropolises were tumbling, too. Copán, with its fine ball court, was under great strain by the end of the eighth century. Tikal, too, went into decline soon after the self-glorification of Ah Cacaw. Why? There have been many theories. It appears that the civilization built on maize foundered on the lack of this most basic commodity. The population of the southern and central lowlands (the area this chapter has concentrated on) had grown dramatically. The demands of the élite would have grown greater and greater in line with their power and grandeur. More and more peasants would have been taken from the land to service an ever- increasing number of élite, and the land would have suffered from the lack of labour and the over-stretching of its natural fertility. There may even have been a drought to exacerbate the situation. Skeletal remains from the period at Copán show signs of severe malnutrition in the great majority of the population. The Maya appear to have outgrown the land and outstripped the food supply. There is evidence of an ecological disaster occurring in the region. The forest had been felled, the land over-farmed and the soil lost through erosion. The drought may have been regional or it might even have been brought about by the loss of tree cover. It is thought that that most powerful symbol of Central America and the Maya, the jaguar, was close to extinction, as was the resplendent quetzal.

The élite, which had grown from the masses, buoyed up by the surplus of maize production, had lost contact with the ecology of the land. One can imagine them bound up in the ritual cycle, looking at the stars for divination, communicating with the gods through blood-letting, and self-absorbed with their power and prestige and the stratagems of war. The situation then declined rapidly. From 751–790, the alliances between cities broke down and a new, more savage warfare emerged. Trade declined, and with it the wealth and power of the élite. New building in the major cities ceased by AD 830. The élite who had made themselves divine, who had exclusively communicated with the gods, and through whose devices the future forces of the universe could be ascertained, were obviously to blame for the spiralling nightmare of disaster. They disappeared, city by city. There are signs in some of the cities that some people stayed on, but there are no commemorative stelae, no new art or architecture, no writing and no calendar dates. The civilization collapsed with the scribes and rulers who had made its observance their life work.

CHAPTER 8

THE TAINO – THE PEOPLE OF THE CARIBBEAN

When Columbus arrived at what he considered to be the east coast of Asia, he was greeted by a group of people who wore little or no clothing. To Columbus these were the people of the Indies; they were 'Indians'. (They became known as Red Indians or, more colloquially, 'red skins' because they decorated their bodies with red plant juices for major ceremonies.) We now know these peoples of the Caribbean as the Taino. Taino means the noble or good people, and it seems to be most appropriate for the Caribbean islanders. They were noble, gentle and hospitable to the first Europeans to arrive on their land. On several occasions the 'native Americans' used the word 'taino' to describe themselves to Columbus. It is now thought that they used the term not as a tribal identity, but to inform the Europeans that they were 'good people' unlike other 'Indians' who lived on the Lesser Antilles.

Long after, the name Taino was applied by scientists to group together the people who spoke the 'Taino' language. The various groups tended to call themselves after the place where they lived. The 'Taino' of the Bahamas, who were the first to see Europeans, called themselves Lucayo (the word means small islands). Those living on Puerto Rico were called Borinquen (the local name for the island). Whether these people of the Caribbean had a name for themselves remains – like so much to do with the Taino – a mystery. The Taino are undoubtedly the most enigmatic of all the cultures of Central America and the Caribbean. They left no great temples, or other masterpieces of architecture, as did the Maya. They had no writing that we know of and, worst of all, within decades of Columbus's arrival the Taino people tragically slipped out of the historic record (see chapter 10). Unlike other native cultures, there is little that has survived the encounter.

Great mystery

The little information we do have about the people of the Caribbean has been hard won and comes from three sources. The first is archaeology. The second is the written records of the Spanish colonists: unfortunately, the Taino disappeared so rapidly after greeting Columbus that there are very few accounts of the people. The third is linguistic: tracing the Taino lexicon back to related tongues to try to discover the history of the language and its speakers. The problem once again is how few words we have to create the connections to other extant languages of the region (see the box on page 165 for Taino words that have transferred into the English language). It is not easy to gain a balanced view of the Taino, but vivid glimpses of limited parts of their world are possible.

PREVIOUS PAGES: The Caribbean coral reefs are home to a myriad colourful fish such as these spotted butterfly fish.

The archaeological evidence paints an unfinished but coherent picture of migration from South America north into the Lesser Antilles, Greater Antilles, Bahamas and, had Columbus not arrived, perhaps further on north into Florida and North America. The archaeologist has the comfort of 'real' physical objects as his or her basic materials. The obverse is that these objects tend to be only what survives long periods of burial: pottery fragments, stone and bone implements, sacred works of art, human bones and remains of meals long since consumed. This is a poor beginning from which to build a picture of a culture and its history. The archaeologist must make inferences, inspired guesses and perform giant leaps of faith to bridge the gap between a piece of pottery and a distant people and their way of life. The problems that scientists face in reconstructing the past are many. They constantly come up against dilemmas such as: are there much older remains, still undiscovered, which will revolutionize our understanding? Was the pottery traded from a separate distant people rather than made locally? If this is so, then no conclusions can be made about local culture. If we follow the scientists and assume with them that their conclusions are correct, then the current archaeological understanding of the Taino is broadly as follows.

The earliest records of ancestral people are from the middle reaches of the Orinoco river. They date from approximately 2000 BC. These people, known from their pottery as the Saladoid, lived in lowland rainforest on the vast flat flood plains of the Orinoco. Their ancestors may have come from either the Amazon or the Andes, the current evidence is inconclusive. The Saladoid pottery people moved down the river, breaking out of the delta between 500 and 300 BC. One group then moved along the coast, while another headed north out into the Caribbean, to become islanders. The pottery of these 'Cedrosan Saladoid people' connects them to their mainland ancestors, and tells us that they kept many of their old continental beliefs and behaviours alive. The figures on the pottery are of wild cats, such as the jaguar, which they revered; and rodents, such as agoutis, which they hunted for food. Neither cats nor agoutis occurred on their new island homes. The Saladoids did not settle on all the islands – only those with high mountains. Here, their pottery remains are found on the north-eastern coasts, where the trade winds unloaded their rain, encouraging lush forests reminiscent of their ancestral homes on the mainland.

After about 1000 years, a change can be discerned in the pottery of the Caribbean, the designs losing their mainland motifs and affinities. The new pottery and its makers are catchily called Ostionoid and the new style is largely plain, with incised lines and often unpainted. It first appears on the island of Puerto Rico and some of its satellite isles, the northern frontier for the earlier Saladoid people. The Ostionoid pottery-makers were not another migration from the mainland, they evolved from the Saladoids in the Caribbean and, unlike the Saladoids, remained isolated from mainland influence. They moved westwards from their Puerto Rico base to populate the other islands of the Greater Antilles, first Hispaniola, then Jamaica and finally, by about AD 1000, Cuba. An offshoot of the Ostionoids migrated out to the Bahamanian archipelago at about the same time. This period of expansion and isolation may mark the transition of the people to true islanders, as the cultural 'memory of the mainland' is lost. After a gap, new, less realistic, more elaborate, symbolic animal decorations appear on the pottery with bats, turtles and frogs becoming important motifs. At the same time as the population was expanding both into the mountainous interior and on to the coast, the remains of many marine creatures turned up in the rubbish heaps. Crabs and turtles, fish and sea snails became important sources of protein.

As early as AD 650 the first structures appeared. They are not villages or houses, but stone-lined precincts which are widely believed to be ceremonial centres. The finest examples have been excavated on Puerto Rico. Tibes, near Ponce on the south coast, boasts a *batey* or ball court and star-shaped ceremonial dance ground. Later, around AD 900, a more elaborate and a larger ceremonial centre was constructed at Caguana in the central cordillera. It is thought to be on the boundary between two chiefdoms, and the ceremonies and ball games may have been conducted by different regional groups. By 1200 the archaeological 'Ostionoid people' are the same as the Taino people known from historical documents.

Languages evolve in a way analogous to cultural artefacts such as pottery. Words change their pronunciation over time. If a group of people are isolated, then the degree of difference in the pronunciation of the same word gives a measure of the relatedness of the two languages, and how long the speakers have been isolated from each other. An example from English is *father*, which is related to the Latin word of the same meaning, *pater*. There are two sites of change of sound, the *p* to *f* and the *t* to *th*. These sound-changes can be analysed into how many basic tongue positions have to change, to move, say, from *p* to *f*. This gives a measure of phonetic distance. The greater the phonetic distance the more remotely related are the two languages. If one more assumption is made – that the rate of phonetic change is roughly constant – then the phonetic distance is also a measure of how long the two languages have been separate. The rather grand name for this linguistic endeavour is 'glottochronological research'.

The results of the language detectives back up the archaeologists' findings. The ancestral language, Proto-Arawakan, arose in the middle Amazon about 3500 BC. From there, Proto-Arawakan speakers moved north up the Rio Negro and across to the head of the Orinoco River. At some point the language evolved into Proto-Maipuran, which itself evolved within the Orinoco drainage into the Proto-Northern. This is calculated from glottochronology at about 100 BC. So it is assumed that the speakers of Proto-Northern were the makers of Saladoid pottery. It is these people who journeyed into the Caribbean to become the Ostionoid potters and Taino speakers encountered by Columbus.

Columbus's *diario*, published by Father Bartolomé de Las Casas, and his report to King Ferdinand and Queen Isabella, are the first Spanish chronicles of the Taino. They record Columbus's observations while he was convinced he was just off the coast of Asia, his mind occupied with the quest for gold and a route to the Far East. While the *diario* may have been re-worded by Columbus's son, or Las Casas, it is still a most valuable eye-witness report, and is referred to extensively in chapter 10 when we look at the changes wrought by European contact. But for the best description of the people of the Caribbean we must look to an uneducated priest.

Father Ramón Pané was a Catalan priest who came to Hispaniola in 1493 as a member of Columbus's second voyage. He was entrusted by Columbus with the task of learning about the Taino religion. His slim work of 26 short chapters is the most comprehensive account we have of the first Native Americans to meet Columbus. It is the original Latin-American literature, based on the first anthropological research in the New World.

The linguists and archaeologists have found strong support for each other's ideas on the journey into the Caribbean. The rest of this chapter will retrace the voyage(s) of the people of the Caribbean. As there are so few material remains of the Taino, compared to the architectural glories of the Classic Maya, the emphasis will be on the world view of the Taino as revealed through the writings of Ramón Pané and brilliantly interpreted by Antonio Stevens-Arroyo.

The Journey

There was probably not one journey but many spread over years, and the end result was a group of people living in the Caribbean. The starting point was the Orinoco River, and the people who live there today give us our best insight into the way of life of the Taino's ancestors. The native peoples, the Yekwana and the Warao, who live along the banks of the Orinoco and its tributaries, have preserved many traditional practices. Aspects of their way of life have remained unchanged for thousands of years, and they still hunt in the forests, and farm small areas around the villages. The Warao live up on the levees, the natural strips of high ground along the river's margins.

The water level of the lower Orinoco rises many metres, causing it to flood every rainy season. For this reason, the Warao build their houses on stilts. This results in nine months of inconvenience, as everything must be laboriously carried up steps and ladders, but this is more than repaid when the houses remain dry above the dark swirling waters of the rising annual flood. The floodwater takes the silt and mud, and drops it over the low-lying flood plains. The bulk of the heavier water-borne particles is deposited close to the river, since the water slows as it penetrates the forest. Over the years the accumulated mud, sand and gravel builds up the levees, the tops of which are only inundated in exceptional floods. These ridges are precious to the Warao of the delta, for they are the only dry land where agriculture can be practised. The Yekwana, who live on a tributary of the middle Orinoco, have more extensive land available for cultivation.

Along the levees the women of the Warao plant their staple crop, known as manioc, cassava, or *yuca*. *Yuca* is a shrub that stores its food in edible swollen roots. In modern dietary parlance, these vitamin-rich tubers are prodigious stores of starch, a carbohydrate and the basic energy source for life. Cassava produces a very heavy crop, compared to other staples such as maize, and is more tolerant of poor soils and hot humid conditions. Two crops a year can be farmed, and the tubers can be stored underground, so that food is available throughout the year. The drawback is that cassava is deadly poisonous. The starch-rich swollen tubers are cassava's bank account, a reserve of energy to be used in next year's growth and expansion. Like a great many plants, cassava protects its investment with 'secondary compounds' to dissuade predators from stealing the plants' precious reserves. Cassava tubers are packed with prussic acid. This is so poisonous that drinking the juice of raw roots is a traditional means of committing suicide!

The Arawakan peoples had the necessary knowledge to overcome the plant's defences and to cash in on the carbohydrate-rich calories. The root is grated and the soggy cassava shavings are squeezed by hand and loaded into a woven wringer. The tube-shaped wringer is stretched to narrow its girth and force out the lethal liquids. The flakes are then laid out on the ground to steam-dry under the tropical sun. Once dry, the chips are pounded into flour. The final stage is to bake bread from the cassava flour. The roughly circular flat loaves are cooked on a griddle over an open fire. The bread keeps well in the humid tropical climate, and can be stored for months.

Cassava supplies most of the calories for the people of the Orinoco, but it does not provide the protein needed for growing bodies. Women are the gardeners, the primary workers, men are the hunters who bring back protein, such as deer and peccaries from the forest. There are also powerful creatures, such as monkeys, with their quasi-human looks and open sexuality; and, most important of all, the jaguar – the supreme hunter that stalks the forests day and night. The creatures of the forest still hold great sway over the people of the Orinoco, and their power on the psyche of the Taino's ancestors would have been just as profound.

Hunting supplies only a part of the protein needs of the Yekwana and Warao, the majority comes from fishing. The rivers and flood-lagoons are full of catfish and characinae, and the Warao feast upon a huge range of them. They fish using bow and spear, and with a poison extracted from a local vine. Fishing with poison is a social event. A small section of a tributary is blocked off and the poison washed into the water. The fish soon appear on the surface, stupefied by the poison. The dying fish are then easily collected by the members of the village.

Throughout history, and most of the world, the highways of commerce and communication have been rivers. The Arawakan people have long been expert canoe-makers. Large trees are selected for the specific canoe required; the tree is then felled and hollowed out, the carving done partly with hand-tools, and partly with fire. A fire lit inside the nascent canoe eats slowly into the surrounding wood of the trunk, enlarging the hollow. The fire-scarred wood is more easily hacked away than raw green timber. In this iterative manner, the canoe emerges from the lumpen trunk: the thick walls become thinner and more elegant, the canoe lighter and capable of carrying greater loads. The heat of the fire softens the wood of the walls of the 'dug-out' canoe. Cross-pieces are forced into position to widen the beam of the craft.

The resulting canoe is a potent piece of technology, capable of travelling great distances along the rivers, and, in the hands of the Taino's ancestors, capable of crossing the open sea to the islands of the Caribbean.

The Taino origin myths
Ramón Pané, the priest sent by Columbus, records two Taino origin myths: both are similar, both imply the importance of the marine world. One is as follows:

There was a man called Yaya, and no one knew his name.
His son was called Yayael, 'Son of Yaya'.
This Yayael was banished for four months.
Afterwards his father killed him, put his bones in a gourd and hung it
from the roof of his house where it hung for some time.
It came to pass that one day, desiring to see his son,
Yaya said to his wife, 'I want to see our son Yayael'.
This made her happy, and taking down the gourd,
she turned it over to see the bones of their son.
From it gushed forth many fish, big and small.
Seeing that these bones had been turned into fishes,
they decided to eat them.

What does the story mean? Stevens-Arroyo makes several major points in his detailed analysis of the myth. The first is that the Taino had a supreme god, Yaya, and his killing of his son signifies patriarchal dominance and power. The myth describes a danger that must have been faced frequently in the history of the Taino. The movement of the ancestors of the Taino on to the Caribbean islands, and the subsequent travel between islands by the Taino themselves, were all motivated by the process of tribal fragmentation. So it should not surprise us that their creation myth talks about this most fundamental process in the history of the Taino.

Why did Yaya kill his son? The splitting of a group would have been along kinship lines. Yayael, who should have departed in search of new resources with his fragment of the clan, returns and is killed by his father. The danger for the Taino is the social tensions and violence that would accompany any such a return, along with the pressure on the natural resources of land and food. So this part of the myth relates a taboo: never return if a village splits and you are cast out. Why do Yaya and his wife eat the bones of their son? This is an obvious reference to cannibalism. The cannibalism here is related to hunger: the people are eating the bones of their children because they have no other food and the children are overburdening the land. This is another reference to the dangers inherent in groups not breaking up and spreading out to new lands. The bones turn into fish emphasizing the importance of marine resources to the Taino. They were a prime source of protein. Moreover, the myth emphasizes the importance of fish in the Taino mind. Yaya's son's bones turn into fish. They are a gift of the gods.

In the second version of the creation myth, quadruplets steal and eat fish from Yaya's gourd. When they hear Yaya returning they try to hang the gourd back up in the rafters, but in their haste drop it. The gourd falls to the ground and smashes, releasing many fish and the waters of the earth, that spread out to form the great ocean *Bagua*.

The meaning of this myth is very similar to the first, but there are differences. The four brothers are stealing fish because they are hungry, again a reference to overtaxing the land. They are swept away by the waters that issue forth from the gourd and form the ocean. This seems like a more obvious statement of the process of migration over the sea – the very process that led to the Taino people. Stevens-Arroyo sees the gourds as canoes that bring the four brothers to earth from the spirit world of the supreme god Yaya.

The ancestors of the Taino would have travelled by canoe out of the Orinoco delta to the coast. We have no idea of how long they might have lived on the coast, but, at some time, they would have paddled out into the Caribbean. The

OPPOSITE: A three-pointed *cemi*. This is Yúcahu, the lord of *yuca* (cassava).

BELOW: The Pitons, St Lucia. Could these dramatic steep-sided mountains have been the original model for the *cemis*? They are certainly awe-inspiring, and would have 'drawn' precious clouds to the islands.

myths suggest that tribal fissure, the natural break-up of a village when it grows too large to be supported by the land, sea, and local resources, set them off. There is little, if any, direct evidence of the route the ancestors took, so conjecture must rule. However, we can be certain that the Taino paddled their canoes because they did not have sails. They would certainly have needed to take note of the sea currents: the North Equatorial Current sweeps east to west, coming from the West African coast across the Atlantic and between the Lesser Antilles into the Caribbean. It would tend to carry the colonists into the void of the Caribbean Sea. How the Taino coped with this problem remains one of the many mysteries surrounding them.

Reconstructed journey?

It is assumed by several academics that the colonists moved up the chain of the Lesser Antilles. This would appear sensible, but not necessary. If they followed the islands, then the first beach they would have reached would have been Trinidad: lush, well-watered and very like the mainland of South America. Geologically, Trinidad and its smaller neighbour, Tobago, are both part of the continent. They were connected by dry land during the Ice Age, so the colonists would have seen animals and plants very familiar to them. There were mammals to hunt in the forests and similar, wild fruiting trees. While on this reassuring outpost of their ancestral homeland, the Taino's ancestors would have tried to discover more about the islands that lay to the north.

The islands of the Caribbean were not uninhabited when the Taino's ancestors, the Saladoid, set off. There were Stone Age people – even less well known than the Taino – living along the coasts of several of the islands. These archaic people – hunters and gatherers, with no agriculture, and little if any art – appear to have moved up from Trinidad on to the Lesser Antilles about 2000 BC, over a thousand years before the Saladoid. On Trinidad, they hunted the mammals of the forests; on the Lesser Antilles, they must have caught fish. The settlements discovered are all along the coast, and many appear to be temporary. Surely the ancestors of the Taino would have learned of the islands and their nature from these shadowy hunters and gatherers. Their fate remains a mystery. We do not know whether they were exterminated in wars, assimilated, or pushed ahead of the wave of invading new islanders.

When the Saladoid people moved out along the chain of the Lesser Antilles, they stepped away from a world that was familiar, one in which their culture had evolved, and into a new maritime realm.

The Lesser Antilles offered new challenges and fresh opportunities to the invading ancestors. They were used to lush, flat, forested lands and giant rivers.

The Lesser Antilles were small, steep and volcanic. The difference must have struck at their imaginations. Some of the first *cemis* (representations of *Taino* deities) are found in this period. It has been suggested that the three-pointed *cemi* reflects the outline of the volcanic islands as seen from the sea. Certainly the *cemis* match the outline of some peaks, such as the Pitons on St Lucia.

The islands posed a serious water problem. The steep-sided mountains have short fast-flowing rivers – very different from the slow giants such as the Orinoco. The rivers shrink, or even stop flowing, in the annual dry season. It may have been for this reason, along with the sense of security that familiarity brings, that the Saladoid settled on the larger, wetter and better forested islands. Inside the forests, the settlers would have felt more at ease, though even here things were subtly different. There were parrots and hummingbirds, but none was the same as back on Trinidad or the mainland. More importantly, there were no large mammals to hunt. In place of the mammals, there were huge numbers of small lizards. The *Anolis* lizards took the ecological place of the small mammals and on some islands there are millions of them. As well as no deer or peccaries there were no carnivores, no jaguars. The islands were decidedly docile compared to the continent.

Food from the sea

The lack of large mammals created a problem. Where were the settlers to find the protein they were accustomed to hunt in the forests? The answer was the sea. The greatest treasure was the manatee. It was slow-moving, defenceless, and lived in shallow inshore waters. This large creature must have been a godsend to the Taino's ancestors. They could feed a village on its meat; its skin could be used to make leather and rope; its bones could be carved into tools and sacred works of art. The most dependable source of protein, though, was the conch. This giant mollusc shared the shallow turtle-grass beds with the manatee, and was simplicity itself to gather. The shell was packed full of meat, relished to this day as a delicacy and an aphrodisiac.

The Taino's ancestors, with their sea-going canoes, were great fishers. They fished by many methods; hook and line, and with nets and traps. The traps depended on the psychology of the reef fish. A woven Z-shaped box was dropped overboard from the canoe to rest on the coral heads of the reef below. Reef fish have a strong sense of security, since there are lots of predators on the reef, and a fish without a home is in trouble. The woven trap offers new accommodation, safety from cruising killers. Fish swim inside to size up their new home, and are unable to find a way out. No bait is needed, just patience, and sure enough 'house-hunting' fish will swim inside.

ABOVE: The conch is a large marine snail that lives in the shallow water of the turtle-grass beds. Here its eyes on the ends of long stalks can be clearly seen.

LEFT: The manatee would have been found throughout the Caribbean, wherever there were shallow vegetation-rich waters. Docile and defenceless, they would have been easy prey for the Taino. Today they are threatened by many of man's activities.

The ancestors of the Taino had plenty of protein sources close by and did not need to go 'deep-sea fishing', but they did, setting out in their canoes in search of the large fast-swimming tuna. They located the schools of these predatory fish by watching their superiors: the fish-eating birds. Wherever noddies and boobies were circling and diving there were shoals of small fish. The birds fed on these and so did the tuna. The water would boil as the tuna dashed through the shoals, and the 'bait fish' leapt from the water in their thousands to escape the jaws of death. These dramatic events would last a few minutes, before the small fish fled to the depths to avoid the predators. Fishermen must have paddled out to these 'feeding frenzies' many times in the hope of catching the tuna during their temporary madness, only to arrive too late, and have to wait until the birds gave the signal again.

The Saladoid people, with their newly honed marine skills, moved north along the Lesser Antilles and out to the Virgin Islands, arriving on present-day Puerto Rico around 200 BC, where we know their descendants became the Ostionoid pottery-makers. Another group of people – named the Island-Caribs – settled in their place on the Lesser Antilles, but, before we continue the story of the journey of the ancestral Taino, we need to look at this related culture.

The Island-Caribs

By the time the Spanish exploration took place, the Island-Caribs were living on the Lesser Antilles, in particular on the more southerly chain, the Windward Islands. *Their* name, rather than that of the Taino, has come to describe the whole region: the Caribbean. Why? The answer is that the Island-Caribs had a reputation. They were considered fierce warriors whom the Spanish described as cannibals.

Columbus, on his second voyage, found himself off the island of Guadeloupe in November 1493, and seized the opportunity to investigate the claims of his Taino guides that the Island-Caribs were cannibals. When his men approached the villages the islanders fled, but they left behind partially dismembered human bodies. The conclusion was that the Island-Caribs were about to eat the flesh of humans for nourishment. (In fact that word cannibal is a corruption of Carib.) In truth it is difficult to know whether the Island-Caribs were cannibals or not. They were supposed to eat parts of their fallen male victims of war. Did they? And, if they did, was it ceremonial rather than a means of gaining useful protein? (Other cultures around the world are recorded as eating their fallen enemies, their parents and so on, to take on some attribute of the ingested, or to interact with the spirit of the dead body.) It is notoriously difficult to prove cases of cannibalism one way or another. It may have suited the Spanish to exaggerate, in order to excuse their own excesses of colonization, and their subsequent mistreatment of the Caribs. Las Casas, the self-appointed protector of the Indians, certainly felt so. He wrote of Columbus's landing on Guadeloupe in 1493:

> *Columbus went ashore and in a house there saw a lot of cotton both woven and ready to be woven, a new kind of loom, and many shrunken heads and bones that must have been the natives' loved ones. It is unlikely that they were remnants of people they had eaten for, if they ate human flesh as much as is said, a house would not accommodate all the bones and heads – which there would be no reason to keep anyway, unless as relics of their most famous enemies, and all this is pure guesswork.*

The Island-Caribs are thought, in one of several competing theories, to be the result of coastal Caribs from Guyana invading the islands around AD 1450. The war-parties colonized the islands and integrated with the local people, a side branch of the Saladoids. The invaders appear to have been young male warriors, who took the local women as brides. The Island-Caribs that resulted from this process spoke the language of the original islanders, but held cultural traditions such as 'bride capture' – the stealing of wives – from neighbouring tribes that originated on mainland South America.

When the Saladoid people arrived at the island of Borinquen, Puerto Rico, they encountered the original inhabitants of the Greater Antilles - the Casimiroid. These were hunter-gatherers, with no known agriculture, who are thought to be responsible for the extinction of the ground sloth, one of the few large mammals that ever made it to the Antilles. The Saladoid were slow to move forward from Puerto Rico to other large islands. They may have spent a long time integrating with the Casimiroids, or, more darkly, it may have taken an age to exterminate the original settlers. The former scenario is suggested by some who believe that the change from Saladoid to Ostionoid was brought about through the influence of Casimiroids incorporated into the ancestral Taino culture.

The flowering of the Taino

The Taino believed that they originated in the Caribbean, that they had always been on these islands, and that they did not arrive as immigrants. This strengthened their sense of ownership, of being the original people. It is apparent that the Taino world was a very ordered one, with many social rules and taboos. Many of their ancient stories or myths both relate to important events in their past and personify social rules. Analogy features strongly as a device, as does the use of 'parables'.

The use of myths as parables that explain what is socially correct behaviour is most clearly seen in the 'Cave of the Jaguar' myth, where the three types of men, the chief, the shaman and the fisherman, each fail to behave as they should, and each in turn is punished. A later part of that myth is as follows:

The shamanic woodpecker

It is said that one day the men went to bathe and while they were in the water, it rained a great deal.
They were very anxious to have women, and on many occasions
while it rained, they had sought to find traces of their women, but they were not able to find any news of them.
But that day when they washed, it is said that they saw fall from some trees, coming down through the branches, a certain kind of persons, who were neither men nor women, nor had the sexual parts of either male or female. When the men went to seize them, they escaped as if they were eels …
After they had captured the creatures, they took counsel about how they could make them women, since they did not have the sexual parts of male or female.
They sought a bird whose name is Inriri, and which in ancient times was called Inriri Cahubabayael.
This bird bores holes in trees, and in our language is called a woodpecker.
Likewise they took the women without the sexual parts of male or female and they tied their hands and feet. They then took this bird and tied it to the bodies.
Thinking that the creatures were logs, the bird began to do the work to which it was accustomed, boring open and pecking away at the place where the female's private is usually found …

This myth has the theme of rain and fertility and female receptivity. There are no women. The eels are of no sex; they are pre-pubertal girls, and this myth tells of their initiation ceremony. The men are *caracaracol*, that is they are syphilitic, and shaman appear often to be afflicted by this disease. The woodpecker is the bird of the shaman and its natural behaviour reflects both the sexual activities of men and initiated women, and perhaps also the shaman's role in the initiation ceremony: one of ritual deflowering. The men then obtain their longed-for women.

The shaman and *cohoba*

Taino society may seem very rule-bound, and, in a sense, this is true. They had social laws and customs that were important in elevating them from the natural world of animals. These rules also kept order in the world. The other notable aspect that comes from studying Taino myths is the importance of the spirit world. It is the mythical and spiritual world that informs the Taino of their culture and its customs. The two come together in the role of the shaman who straddled the world of humans and the world of spirits.

The shaman's role in Taino society, as in most native American cultures, is a central one – his power coming from his privileged access to another world. Able to communicate with the spirit world to discover the nature of things unknown and unseen, his task, as healer, comes from his position as conduit with spirits that may be causing illness. The Taino shaman used an hallucinogenic powder, *cohoba*, to aid his contact with the world of spirits. *Cohoba* is made of the ground-up seeds of a native tree and the powder is inhaled as a snuff. Once the shaman was in contact with the spirit world he could interrogate them on behalf of the sick person whose body they had entered. He also fulfils the same role when he officiates in puberty rites, acting as intermediary between the natural world of the girls and the religious symbolic world that will bring them fertility. His totemic animals had the same ability; and the woodpecker, mentioned above, was a creature of the sky and of the earth.

Cemis

It was taboo for the Taino to walk in the forest at night. This was because the spirits of the dead were active at night, and took the form of bats and owls. The day was the world of the living, the night the place of the dead. The world was divided into opposites: night and day; spirits of the dead and the living; men and women; remoteness (sexually unavailable) and closeness (fertile and receptive); rainy season and dry season. Here once again the orderliness of the Taino understanding of the world is very apparent. In their *cemis*, or spirits, it is even clearer.

Fernandina's flicker, a woodpecker endemic to Cuba. The woodpecker was the Taino shaman's bird.

The tradition of making *cemis* goes back to the Saladoids, the ancestors who first voyaged into the blue Caribbean. The use of *cemis* is the most distinctive aspect of Taino religious life. Many of their myths can be traced back to related cultures in South America, but *cemi*-ism evolved on the Caribbean islands.

The Taino ancestors carved small three-pointed stones. Over time these became larger and more elaborate, and often had faces of humans and animals, as well as legs and geometric patterns.

One kind of three-pointed carved stone represents the spirit, Yúcahu, whose name translates as 'lord of the *yuca*'. The *cemi* was buried when the root crop was planted to increase the yield. On the carved stones, Yúcahu has his mouth open to ingest the soil, so creating room for the swelling *yuca* tuber. The *cemis* are spirit intermediaries between Yaya, the supreme god, and mortals. They are lower-ranking spirits and specific to certain roles; as in the case of Yúcahu, the fertility and growth of *yuca*.

Father Ramón Pané, the first chronicler of Taino religion, mentions a comical case of cultural misunderstanding. After the *cemi* was planted along with the crop, the Taino would urinate over the ground. Whether this was considered of practical value for watering and fertilizing the new planting, or purely symbolic, we do not know. However, some of the early Taino converts to the Catholic Church were given small statues of the saints, and, understanding them to be spirit intermediaries, analogous to their own *cemis*, proceeded, to the great horror of the Spanish priest in attendance, to bury them and urinate upon them!

There are *cemis* of daily weather that help the growth of crops such as *yuca*, but not all were beneficial, there are spirits of destruction, too. The *cemis*, in fact, are in two opposing groups, those who are fruitful, and those who are destructive. This again reflects the tidiness and symmetry in the Taino mind, and is reminiscent of the division into day and night, living and dead. The Taino cosmos was composed of contrasting pairs. Fertility and destruction were the complementary forces of life. The Taino ensured the orderliness of their cosmos by ceremonies and dances, called *arietos*. These kept their realm of culture separate from the chaos of the natural world. By ceremonies, the Taino kept the balance between the spirits of destruction and fruitfulness. The ball game they played was similar to the Maya's, the result determining which of the life forces would triumph. The game, like the dances, was a means of divining and trying to control the future.

The people who greeted Columbus

That future for the Taino was to include the dubious honour of being the first Native Americans to greet Columbus. The Taino religion, which intricately interweaved the spiritual with the natural world, was no match for the materialistic greed of the adventurer Spaniards. The Taino resistance, it has been argued, was largely spiritual, depending on the *cemis* of destruction to determine the fate of the Spanish invaders. The Taino had evolved a culture, separate from the great cultures of mainland Mexico. On their remote islands they had grown by tribal splitting; war was not an integral part of their culture. These people of the Caribbean, in the security of isolation, had grown into a peaceful, highly spiritual culture, fashioned from the nature of their island home. In the populous highlands of Mexico lived a group of people whose reputation could not be more different: the Aztecs, the greatest military power of the Americas.

Taino words

Batata – our potato, which is now applied to the Peruvian bitter root. Originally, *batata* referred to the sweet potato of the Caribbean.

Canoa – our canoe. The *canoa* was a dug-out boat of any size. It was made, typically, from the trunks of silk-cotton trees. These are giants that can grow to 30 metres high. Early Spanish accounts describe some as big enough for 50 paddlers.

Casabe – the unleavened bread made from *yuca* flour; our cassava.

Hamac – our hammock and certainly a Taino word. This was the typical bed, strung up outside or inside their *caney* or house.

Huracan – the *cemi* or spirit of wild winds. Our hurricane.

Iwana – our iguana, the large lizard of Central and South America.

Maiz – maize or corn, the staple diet for most of the Americas, but not the Taino who depended more upon *yuca*, manioc or cassava.

Maraca – the musical instrument much beloved by folk and rock bands. It is made of a gourd with small rocks inside. The Taino used it at their *arietos* (ceremonies and dances).

Nagua – name for female loincloth. The length was a measure of the married woman's status and rank. The name is alive and still used in Puerto Rico for slips or underskirts.

Tabaco – our tobacco and one of Columbus's 'gifts' to the Old World. Some scholars argue that tobacco comes from an Arabic word *tarriq*.

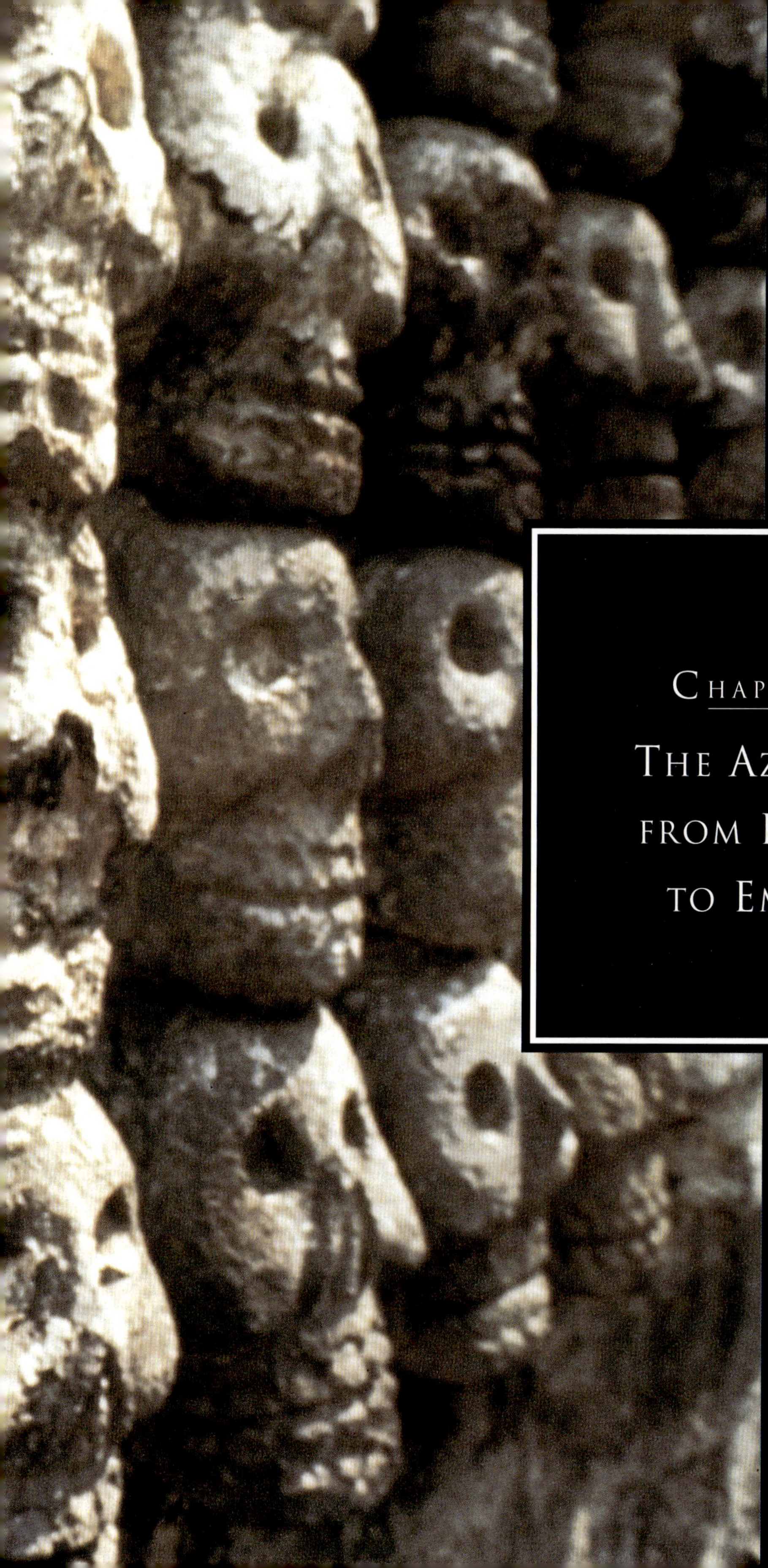

CHAPTER 9

THE AZTECS – FROM DESERT TO EMPIRE

The Aztecs are just one of the many cultures that sprang up in Mexico as a consequence of the domestication of maize. Yet they are one of a small number of cultures in the world that are 'household names'. Why are the Aztec so famous, or infamous, in comparison to the other peoples of America? Part of the answer is the gripping account of the encounter between the tough Spanish conquistador, Hernán Cortés, and the Aztecs in 1521, but the main reason must be their reputation as fierce warriors. They are lodged in the common psyche as the people who ceremonially sacrificed thousands of victims by ripping out their hearts. To understand how a people came to believe their existence depended on such mass blood-letting, we will follow the history of the Aztecs, up to their fateful first encounter with Europeans.

The Aztecs appear very late on the scene in Central America. The great flowering of the Maya had already passed when a group of 'savages' began to migrate south from the wild country of northern Mexico. What we know of the Aztecs comes from their own histories and from early Spanish chroniclers. Neither can be wholly trusted because both reflect the obvious bias of the recorder; the Aztec scribes, in particular, glorified their leaders, judiciously rewriting history, and so increasing their importance. But in comparison to other cultures of the region, particularly the Taino, there is a great deal recorded about the Aztecs, and ethnographers and historians have been able to piece together a portrait that is a reasonable likeness of the people.

They came from a place called 'Aztlan', which translates from Nahuatl, the language of the Aztecs, as 'the Land of the White Herons'. The Aztecs gain their name from this place. Where is it? We do not know exactly, but it was an island in a lake somewhere in western or north-western Mexico. The white herons may well have been white cranes, far more majestic and noteworthy birds, that would have appeared in the sky each winter, having flown south from their breeding grounds. The cranes performed their courtship dances in spring before mysteriously flying off to the north. Whooping cranes are now very rare and confined to a small wintering area along the northern fringes of the Gulf of Mexico. But were they much more widely distributed in the time of the Aztecs?

The Aztecs say they set off from Aztlan in AD 1111. Ruled by tribal chieftains and with no writing, architecture or art that we know of, they were not a civilized people. Their deity was Huitzilopochtli, 'the Hummingbird on the Left', a fierce god of war, and it is he who led them. The Aztec story has Huitzilopochtli giving

PREVIOUS PAGES: The *tzompantli*, the Aztec skull rack. The plinth of carved skulls was most likely surmounted by racks of the skulls of human sacrificial victims.

the people a new name during their journey. They were to be called the *Mexica* from which the modern country takes its name. Along the way, they stopped at a cave from which emerged all the people who were to make up the *Mexica*. These mythical events lend gravitas to the Aztec leader, this is their history, their ancestry traced to a deity; their rationale for ruling with a group of allies.

Why did the Aztecs leave Aztlan? We do not know, but there appear to have been problems in the northern 'wastelands', the land of uncivilized people, the Chichimeca, of which the Aztecs were but a small and insignificant part. It might have been warfare, it might have been a regional drought. The northern lands are still largely arid and barren, deserts of several kinds. These are marginal lands to work in the hope of agricultural return. Here people must be flexible, able to adapt to the uncertain rainfall, to move in search of food. The deserts are neatly characterized as lands of dust, spiny cactus and venomous animals. Some of the harshness of these wastelands must have rubbed off on to the Aztec character.

Whatever the cause, many bands of Chichimeca appear to have migrated south and settled in the northern half of the Valley of Mexico, which still had its great interconnected lakes. The more fertile southern half was already occupied by the remnants of the great Toltec civilization, which had ended with the destruction of Tula, their capital, in the twelfth century.

The Valley of Mexico

When the Aztecs arrived, in the early part of the fourteenth century, the valley was already full of people. The Aztecs were seen as an unwanted bunch of uncouth nomads. They seem to have faced a similar prejudice as the Gypsies suffer throughout Europe. Wherever they went they were on someone else's land, reviled for stealing wives from the civilized city folk, and harried and chased from one patch of land to another. They worked as serfs, their legend tells us, eating vermin and snakes; a terribly degrading description for any people.

In 1323, over 200 years after they left their lakeland of Aztlan, they finally settled on some swampy, remote islands in the great, marsh-rimmed, shallow Lake Texcoco, 'The Lake of the Moon'. The Aztecs had travelled with a prophecy that they would finally settle when they saw an eagle perched atop a prickly-pear cactus, holding a snake in its beak. Once the eagle had been sighted the Aztecs built their city, Tenochtitlán.

In 1367 the humble Aztecs became mercenaries of the Tepanec kingdom, based around the city of Atzcapotzalco. The Tepanec were rapidly conquering the other city-states in the Valley of Mexico. The Aztecs grew in sophistication under the rule of the Tepanec, and, in 1428, the new Aztec 'king', Itzcoatl, 'Obsidian Snake', led them in revolt. They conquered the Tepanec and destroyed the city of

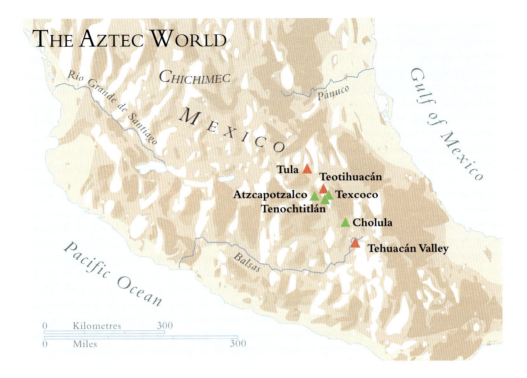

The Aztec World

Atzcapotzalco. The Aztecs assumed control of the largest empire in Mexico, ruled from Tenochtitlán. This was only the start, but first the full glory and importance of the Aztecs had to be assured.

Huitzilopochtli, the Aztec sun god

The chief advisor to Itzcoatl was Tlacaelel, and, following the Aztecs' initial success, he rewrote the history books. First he destroyed the books that recorded the history of the vanquished enemies, and then he created a tribal history that made the Aztecs the chosen people, whose role it was to keep order in the world. The eagle on the cactus as a prophecy, which legitimized the founding of Tenochtitlán, is most likely an addition at the hand of Tlacaelel. Another piece of refining of tribal history increased the importance of the Aztecs through their tribal god Huitzilopochtli.

A pause was fabricated on the great journey to their present island. The place was Coatepec, 'Snake Mountain', near the ruins of the ancient city of the Toltecs, Tula. The Aztec tribal god, Huitzilopochtli, is reborn as the sun god. The myth, in good Aztec fashion, is exciting, action-packed and not short of spilled blood. One version goes as follows: The goddess Coatlicue, 'She of the Serpent Skirt', is sweeping up at Snake Mountain, when she comes across a bundle of feathers.

Coatlicue tucks them into her waistband so as to save the precious objects for later. But when she comes to look for them, they have disappeared. The ball of feathers has impregnated her! As time goes by her body swells as Huitzilopochtli grows inside her. Now her other children, the 400 southerners, and Coyolxauhqui, Huitzilopochtli's half-sister, notice that their mother is pregnant. They feel shame and decide to kill her. Coatlicue learns of her childrens' plan and is terrified, but the unborn Huitzilopochtli talks to his mother from the womb, calming her fears. The goddess's children approach her on the mountain top and chop off her head, but not before Huitzilopochtli is born fully armed. He attacks his sister Coyolxauhqui with his 'Tourquoise Serpent', a weapon of fire, pierces her chest and cuts off her head. Her dismembered body tumbles to the bottom of Snake Mountain.

What does it mean? The birth of Huitzilopochtli is the birth or dawn of the sun. His fiery weapon with which he kills his sister is the rays of the sun that drive away the darkness of night. Coyolxauhqui may be the Milky Way or the moon, while her 400 brothers are the night stars that are overwhelmed each dawn by the bright rays of the sun. The fierceness of the characters and the violence of

---

The northern desert of Mexico, the wasteland of the Chichimec.
This is the land that tempered the Aztecs' world view.

the portrayal of dawn, of the birth of the sun, speak volumes for the Aztec mind-set. As well as telling of the birth of the sun, this myth serves to validate the Aztec conquest of the other people of the Valley of Mexico. Just as their god Huitzilopochtli had destroyed and scattered his elder siblings and his sister, so the upstart Aztecs had conquered the established people of the valley.

Much of the Aztecs' future way of life revolved around satisfying this fierce god. The Aztecs' history of suffering both the vagaries of climate and other more powerful foes seems to have created a strong sense of anxiety, a cosmic neurosis. They knew that there had been other cultures that had vanished, the abandoned metropolises of Tenochtitlán and Tula were nearby, and so they must have felt that their nascent empire was threatened with a similar future.

The Aztec calendar emphasized the cyclic nature of time, and it was now the time of the Aztecs, but without their active intervention and constant sacrifices that time would come to an end. Their emphasis was different from other cultures that felt a responsibility to offer the gods gifts as a 'thank you' for past or future blessings. In the case of the Aztecs it seems more like a compulsive need to continue offering the gods gifts simply to keep the world functioning. Without such sacrifices the world would stop. It was the Aztecs who had to keep their warlike sun god, Huitzilopochtli, travelling across the sky. Dawn was not a serene event, the Aztecs saw it as a violent struggle, with an uncertain outcome: the sun only overcomes darkness by killing his sister. Just as Huitzilopochtli's weapon, the fiery serpent Xiuhcoatl, was driven into the chest of his sister, Coyolxauhqui, so the beating hearts of victims were ripped from their chests. Aztec sacrifices were needed if the sun was to rise again from the darkness.

Huitzilopochtli demanded the hearts of victims if he was to rise the next morning. This speech to a new-born boy child reflects the prime role of an Aztec: ' … your mission is to give the sun the blood of enemies to drink, and to feed Tlaltecuhtli, the earth, with their bodies'. The hearts of enemy warriors were needed and wars were fought not only for conquest *per se*, nor just for new lands, but for fresh hearts.

The Empire

The Aztecs (the *Mexica*) soon set out to conquer new lands, and capture new hearts. Motecuhzoma Ihuilcamina (also known as Montezuma and Moctezuma), who ruled from 1440 to 1469, led the Aztecs into a great expansion of their empire. He created an alliance between the three city-states of Tenochtitlán, Texcoco and Tlacopan. Motecuhzoma then instigated a phoney conflict, the so-called 'Flowery War'. This was permanent and fought out between the Aztec allies and two nearby states. The sole purpose of the Flowery War was to capture prisoners for sacrifice. But there were 'serious' wars. Under Motecuhzoma, the Aztecs took the lands to the north-east, the home of the Huaxteca. Ahuizotl, 1486–1502, was the greatest of the warrior leaders. Under his rule, the Aztec empire reached out and embraced most of central Mexico: from the northern wastelands of the uncivilized Chichimeca, it stretched as far south as the border of present-day Guatemala.

War was the principal activity of the Aztec Empire. Everyone was expected to fight, even the priests. The Aztec weapons were brutally effective, if not overly sophisticated. There was a wooden club with edges lined with razor-sharp obsidian blades. There were spears and darts that were launched from the *atatl*, the weapon used by the mammoth-hunters, 10 000 years earlier. (*Atatl* is an Aztec word, which has come to be used to describe all spear-launchers.) The warriors dressed in the skins of jaguars or eagle-feathered suits, their appearance designed to strike terror, and carried shields of hide decorated with the multicoloured hues of tropical bird feathers. The state's aim was to expand the empire and gain more tribute, so the warrior's aim was not to kill but to capture as many enemy warriors as possible. The captives were destined to be sacrificed – all warriors believed they would die gloriously on the field of battle or as sacrificial victims. To do so was to avoid the underworld of the dead and, instead, be transformed into a hummingbird and travel directly to join the sun god in paradise.

It seems a curious paradox that such a warlike people should have written fine poetry, but the Aztecs did, and much of it about war:

> *There is nothing like death in war,*
> *nothing like the flowery death*
> *so precious to Him who gives life:*
> *far off I see it: my heart yearns for it!*

The above poem, translated by Dr Michael Coe, glorifies the central tenet of Aztec life – warfare. To die for Huitzilopochtli was to die with distinction.

Trade and tribute

The Aztec Empire was organized into provinces with military outposts and governors, and each province had to pay tribute to the Valley of Mexico. In the time of the second Motecuhzoma, the empire was supplying nearly 20 000 tons of food, mainly maize. More impressive still were the two million cotton capes (cotton did not grow in the highland Valley of Mexico). On top of that were luxury items, such as amber, jade and gold, as well as military costumes and feathered shields and headdresses. Much of this went into the state coffers to pay

the huge hierarchy of workers, and to increase the grandeur of the palaces and temples. Some of the goods, however, found their way on to the open market.

There were vast daily markets in Tenochtitlán. Here, carefully policed by inspectors, over 60 000 people traded goods and food from all over the empire and beyond.

Quetzal feathers came from the cloud-covered highlands far to the south. Amber came from the present-day province of Oaxaca. Jade was brought from the Mayan lowlands. Cacao beans, from the lowlands, were so precious that they formed a rudimentary currency – a tradition inherited from the Maya. Their high cost meant that only the élite could afford to consume chocolate. The beans were used to make chocolate drinks flavoured with vanilla or even chili. The finest pottery and turquoise mosaic masks came from the enemy city of Cholula, and slaves were transported from Atzcapotzalco. The city was the centre of a vast web of trading and tribute routes that fed the wealth of the empire.

The Aztec king Ahuizotl set about major civic improvements at the island city of Tenochtitlán, as befitted the capital of an empire of as many as 10 million souls. Tenochtitlán – covering 45 square kilometres – was undoubtedly one of the greatest cities in the world in the sixteenth century. It is estimated to have had a population of between 200 000 and 300 000, five times larger than the London of Henry VIII. It was reached by long thin causeways across the lake, one of these over five kilometres in length. The Aztecs had no large domestic animals, so the causeways had no need to be wide, and were designed for foot-traffic only. The causeways were a conduit for tribute from all over the empire.

The main cargo was food from the *chinampas* – 'floating' gardens set in the lake; these still exist and are actively farmed to the south of Mexico City. The maize, beans, squashes and chilies were brought both as tribute and to be bartered in the great marketplace. The *chinampas* are not unique to the Aztecs, but, with typical vigour, these people were able to produce a large proportion of the produce necessary for the metropolis. Water-weeds, vegetation and the smelly but rich mud from the bottom of the lake are piled up to create a well fertilized if wet garden plot. A channel is formed where the weeds and mud were extracted. Willow trees are planted along the edges, and, over the years, repeated dredging and dumping create a maze of pockets of dry land and canals. The peasant class lived on their *chinampas*, in houses constructed of reeds and mud with thatched roofs. The *chinampas* were intensely fertile, fed on the decaying ooze from the bottom of the canals.

The canals also produced food. *Axalotls*, large immature salamanders, unique to the lakes, were considered a delicacy. Tadpoles also fed the people of the great city. Insect eggs were specially harvested in their millions. This is a tradition that has survived to modern times, and is only now succumbing to the pressures of hamburger uniformity. Sheaves of long-stemmed grasses are placed in the shallow opaque olive waters, providing the substrate for the insects to lay their eggs. The eggs are then stripped from the stems and collected. Alongside the insect eggs, adults and larvae were also gathered. While insects may not appeal to the modern palate, they were important sources of protein then.

The lakes provided another rich food source that may be even more off-putting to us. Scum was skimmed from the lakeshore and compressed into 'cakes'. This 'scum' was, in fact, a primitive alga called *Spirulina*, which today's scientists are investigating as a protein-rich food source to alleviate the malnutrition of parts of the Third World. The lakes also provided more conventional fare in the form of fish and waterfowl, but these were for the élite. The lakes were a haven for thousands of wintering ducks and waders, and, even today, the small remnant of the lake still attracts water birds.

The city was laid out in a grid pattern and divided into quarters. The channels that defined the *chinampas* ran north and south, with other big canals running east and west. In the centre of the city were the houses of the élite, the merchants, craftsmen and artisans, clerks and priests. Their houses were constructed of adobe bricks with flat roofs – a style of architecture still practised today. The most important royal palaces and buildings were in the centre of the town surrounding the Sacred Precinct (see below). Among them were the Emperor's gardens, zoo and aviary. The aviary was no small affair: there were ten large rooms which held both salt and fresh water. The Emperor had birds brought from all corners of the Aztec Empire. The only bird the Aztecs could not keep, supposedly, was the magnificent quetzal, perhaps because of its specialized diet of wild avocados. The zoo held the fierce wild beasts of the highlands and lowlands including foxes, pumas and the great jaguar.

The temples

In the epicentre was the Sacred Precinct, which contained the religious buildings, and was surrounded by the *coatepantli*, the 'Snake Wall'. The largest building inside the walls was the Great Temple. This was really two temples, one to Huitzilopochtli, the other to that ubiquitous Central American deity, the rain god, Tlaloc. The temple had twin stairways, one for each god, and both were darkened by the congealed blood of human sacrifice. At the base of the steps that led to the temple of Huitzilopochtli lay a magnificent sculpted stone depicting the broken body of the sun god's sister, Coyolxauhqui. After the heart was ripped out of a sacrificial victim, the body was thrown down the steep stairs, replicating the action in the great myth of the sun god banishing the darkness and night stars. The lifeless body would have landed upon the great carved stone at the base of the stairs.

The great god Tezcatlipoca, the god of war and patron god of the Emperor, and Tezcatlipoca's brother and adversary, Quetzalcoatl, god of life and culture, and the patron of the priests, both had temples inside the precinct, as did Xipe Totec, 'The Flayed One', god of springtime. The walled precinct of temples was considered the centre of the universe. It was the scene of a panoply of colourful celebrations, enacted throughout the year.

The Almanac calendar dictated the particular rituals to be performed by the priests. The two calendars, the solar and Almanac, realigned every 52 years. The end of the 'Calendar Round' (see chapter 7) was considered a very dangerous time when the world could be destroyed. So, every 52 years on the very last day, all fires in Tenochtitlán were put out and the priests waited to see if the alignment of the stars was correct at midnight. If it was, then the uncertain Aztec world would continue. To celebrate, a fire was started inside the freshly opened chest of a captive warrior, and the flame was then carried out to all corners of the empire: a new flame, new light to shine on the next Calendar Round.

In some ceremonies men impersonated Xipe Totec by wearing the skins of flayed victims. Only when the 20 days of the month, *tlacaxipehualiztli*, were over was the priest able to take off the skin, by which time it had reached an advanced, highly odorous state of decomposition. The bizarre yet apt metaphor of a flayed skin for spring seems quintessentially Aztec: from death and macabre horror life is reborn. While the priest 'dressed' as Xipe Totec may have been a very bizarre sight, the celibate priesthood, highly trained and well versed in the complex web of daily rituals, was, in general, eye-catchingly odd to look at. Their long hair was clotted with the blood of sacrifices; their ears and penises shredded from the many times they had let blood using a stingray spine or agave thorn; and they smelled of decomposing flesh and blood.

The metropolis of Tenochtitlán. One of the greatest cities of its time. The causeways and central temple precinct are clearly visible.

The human sacrifices

Captured warriors were washed and ceremonially cleansed, before ascending the stone steps to the temple proper. There, the victims were stretched out over the sacrificial stone, their chests sliced open with a ceremonial obsidian blade, and the exposed heart ripped out. This heart was offered to the gods in a vessel. The walls of the temple were splattered and stained deep red-black by the congealed blood of the victims. The human hearts and blood were burnt, and the black smoke rose to the gods. The stench must have been stupefying. The blackness of the smoke was symbolic of volcanoes and the god, Black Tezcatlipoca, 'the Smoking Mirror'.

How many were sacrificed? Here the bias of observers comes into play again. The Spaniards, for example, wanted to paint as black a picture as possible of barbaric savages, so as to excuse their own terrible excesses (see next chapter). The figure often mentioned is 80 000 war captives executed for the dedication of the great temple in 1487. Nowadays, scholars tend to play down the numbers, though there is no doubt that hundreds and probably thousands of people were sacrificed each year.

The Aztec pantheon

The Aztec religion and myths give a clear insight to their way of thinking. Some of their gods can be traced to other Mexican cultures, but the myths emphasize uncertainty and the cycle of destruction and rebirth in a

characteristically Aztec manner. The supreme deity was Ometeotl, a god of duality with both male and female characteristics. One aspect of the female side was Coatlicue, 'Serpent Skirt', mother of Quetzalcoatl. Ometeotl ruled through lesser deities, created from the god's bisexual nature, or perhaps just aspects of him-herself. She-he lived in the highest of 13 heavens, while the other gods, the four Tezcatlipocas, dwelled in the lower layers, and below them were the celestial deities, the stars, moon and milky way. The four Tezcatlipocas were each aligned with a compass direction and a colour. The Black Tezcatlipoca of the north was 'Smoking Mirror', the god of war, and the dispenser of life and riches. He could see into hearts by means of his obsidian mirror. This 'talent' is associated with the jaguar who can see in the night because its eyes are naturally mirrored, with their reflective rear surface, the *tapetum*. Also, like Aztec warriors – some of whom were called 'jaguar knights' – the jaguar is thought of as a supreme predator, as was 'Smoking Mirror'.

Quetzalcoatl, lord of life and human culture, was the White Tezcatlipoca of the east. The Blue Tezcatlipoca of the south was Huitzilopochtli, the Aztec's own warrior god of the sun, who required human hearts and blood if he was to rise again after his night-time journey through the underworld. The last Tezcatlipoca was the red one from the east. He was Xipe Totec, 'Our Lord the Flayed One', the god of spring. The flayed human skin symbolized the rebirth of the land and the re-covering of the land with green after the rains.

Below the earth there were nine layers of the underworld, overseen by Mictlantecuhtli (the God/Lord of the underworld) and through these layers permeated the souls of the dead. Only warriors who died in the field of battle, sacrificial victims and women who died in childbirth went up to the celestial heavens.

The Aztec creation myth

The Aztecs, like other Central American peoples, believed there had been other worlds before the present one. In the case of the Aztecs there had been four. The Black Tezcatlipoca, 'Smoking Mirror', is lord of the first world, which is peopled by giants. Quetzalcoatl and his brother, Tezcatlipoca, fight over the world, and in the process the giants are destroyed. The Aztecs knew of giant bones found near the ancient city of Teotihuacán. They were the bones of mammoths killed by the first hunters of Mexico, 7000 years before. It is intriguing to speculate that they connected these bones with the lost giants of

PREVIOUS PAGES: The 'floating' gardens or *chinampas* which are still farmed today.
The banks of the artificial islands are held in place by willow trees.

the first world. Quetzalcoatl is the ruler of the next world. This time Tezcatlipoca wins the struggle with Quetzalcoatl, and the world is swept away by winds; the descendants of the hapless humans of this world are thought to be monkeys. The third world is presided over by the rain god, Tlaloc. Quetzalcoatl destroys this world in a rain of fire — most likely a reference to volcanic eruptions, a terrifying and not uncommon event in the Valley of Mexico. The people of this world are turned into turkeys.

The goddess of streams, Chalchiuhtlicue, the wife of Tlaloc, is ruler of the fourth world, which is destroyed by a great flood. The people then turn into fish as the world is washed away by the flood water and the unsupported heavens crash down. (The destructive force of floods and landslides must have been well known to the Aztecs in their fertile but precarious home. The Valley of Mexico looks out on volcanoes, and suffers floods, droughts and earthquakes. The vagaries of the valley are reflected in the myth of creation, and destruction.)

The fifth, the present world, is made by the violent sons of the dual god, Quetzalcoatl and Tezcatlipoca, whose fighting had destroyed the prior worlds. They create the heavens and the earth from the body of Tlaltecuhtli, the earth monster, who appears as a giant caiman. The scaly back of this monster rises out of the water, and the spines become the ridges of the mountains of the Aztec world. This earth monster myth was common in Central American cultures, and one Aztec version sheds more light on their relationship to the land. In this story, the dismembered body of Tlaltecuhtli furnishes the features of the earth: her skin and hair become the plants and trees, her nose and mouth, the caves and caverns, and her eyes, the springs and wells. At night, the earth goddess is heard screaming for the blood and hearts of people — only this can calm the earth, and allow her body to be fruitful. What were the noises of the earth monster? Volcanic rumblings, landslides, earthquakes?

The fifth world was without people. Quetzalcoatl takes the bones of the fish people of the prior world, the land of the dead. These bones are then ground into a flour for the gods to spill their own blood on to. From this mix come the people of the fifth world. Now the gods needed a sun to light their new world and its people. The Aztecs believed the sun was created, and time began, at Teotihuacán, 'the place of those who became gods', a vast ancient city to the north east of Tenochtitlán.

It is told that when yet all was in darkness, when yet no sun had shone and no dawn had broken — it is said — the gods gathered themselves together and took counsel amongst themselves there at Teotihuacán. They spoke; they said among themselves:

'Come hither, O gods! Who will carry the burden? Who will take it upon himself to be the sun, to bring the dawn?'

The diseased god, Nanahuatzin, immolates himself in the flames of the sacrificial fire. He is followed by the god, Tecuciztecatl, and the eagle and jaguar. The tips of the eagle's feather are scorched black, while the jaguar sports the smudges from the fire. Because of their bravery the eagle and jaguar are the knights of war, and Aztec warriors dressed for battle in their pelts and feathers. Nanahuatzin appears flaming red above the eastern horizon, transformed into the sun to light the fifth world. Then Tecuciztecatl appears in the east, too. Fearing that two suns will scorch the new earth, the gods throw a rabbit at the face of the second god. The rabbit lands and dims the light; so the moon was created, with the mark of a rabbit imprinted on its face. The sun god then demands the blood of the remaining gods before he will travel across the sky. Infuriated at the arrogance of the new sun, Tlahuizcalpantecuhtli, the god of

OPPOSITE: Xipe Totec, the 'Flayed One', the god of spring renewal. This brilliant, if gruesomely realistic, sculpture shows the god dressed in the facial and body skin of a sacrificial victim.

BELOW: Teotihuacán, the ancient city of the Mexican highlands, and in Aztec legend the site of the birth of the fifth world.

the morning, the morning star, fires a dart at the sun but misses. The sun fires back and pierces the morning star's head. Tlahuizcalpantecuhtli is turned to cold stone. This is why it is always cold in the morning.

There may be more to this story, for in the deserts of Mexico, the Aztecs' homeland, there is a phenomenon called 'the breath of god'. Each night it becomes very cold, for the air is dry and thin and there are no clouds to act as a blanket and keep the earth's heat in. In the hours before dawn it is cold and still, but as the sun creeps up towards the horizon its rays are already striking the air above. The air heats up and rises. Cold air is sucked in to replace the rising air above. The result is a chilling ice-cold wind that appears from nowhere and rushes over the land. Once the sun is above the horizon, its rays warm the ground and the 'breath of god' departs. Is the dart fired by the sun god, the sun's rays and the icy wind? In the myth, the gods eventually give in to the sun god's demands. They all rip out their hearts, sacrificing themselves so that people can have day and night. Just as the gods, humans too must give up their hearts and blood to ensure that the sun will rise again to light the world.

The Aztec world view was a very sophisticated one: they were no savages. They saw the world as uncertain and dangerous. The events of the natural world were portrayed as battles and wars, violence coloured their views of all events. They lived in a valley that was prone to the cataclysmic actions of volcanoes and earthquakes. It was a world that had been populated before by giants – there were deserted cities to prove it. There was no permanence. Civilizations had come and gone, and the Aztecs felt that theirs was also vulnerable, particularly at the end of a 52 year round.

The end of the Empire

Imagine the scene, then, as the Emperor Motecuhzoma Xocoyotzin receives portents and prophecies. The first, a comet, travelled across the sky upsetting the balance of sun and moon, day and night. Then the Emperor hears soothsayers tell of men wearing clothes of black stone and mounted on deer without antlers who will arrive at the capital and destroy it. Then, in 1518, a messenger arrives from the coast of the Gulf of Mexico with wild stories of mountains moving on the waters, while, in 1519, houses are seen moving on the sea, from which men with pale faces and beards emerge. This seemed to fit the story of the return of Tyopitzin Quetzalcoatl, the demi-god and ruler of the Toltec people, who had disappeared to the 'red lands to the east' over 500 years before. One of the men seen emerging was Hernán Cortés, a Spanish conquistador and adventurer and the nemesis of the Aztec Empire, but that is another story and another chapter.

Part III

FIVE HUNDRED
YEARS OF CHANGE

Chapter 10
East meets West

For hundreds of years Columbus was the archetypal heroic explorer. In recent decades Columbus's achievements have been re-evaluated. It is true that he set out to find another route to China and Cipango (Japan). His motivation was fame and fortune. It is true that he failed in this mission and never really came to terms with the fact that he had discovered, or stumbled upon, a 'New World' – the Americas – which was new only from a European perspective, given that Native American peoples had lived there for at least 13 000 years! To them, it was *the* world, *their* world, how could Columbus 'discover' it? Whatever his shortcomings, Columbus was a single-minded, bold explorer and an excellent navigator. His 'discovery', his encounter with the people of the Americas, changed the world for both Europeans and Native Americans. For the Taino it spelt doom.

The small fleet of three boats left Spain on Friday, 3 August 1492, heading for the Canary Islands as a staging post. On 6 September, Columbus departed Gomera and headed out into the great Atlantic. The three ships were sailing out into the unknown. Sailors' stories abounded of what the sea was like, of large islands in the middle of the ocean, of sea monsters, but all was rumour and supposition.

Columbus kept a diary or log of his voyages. On Monday, 17 September, he records that there was a great deal of weed. The sailors reckoned they must be close to land, but they were wrong and still far from land. They had sailed into the Sargasso Sea and were looking at sargassum weed, which spends its whole life circling around the great gyre in the midst of the North Atlantic. The three boats sailed through the weedy masses of the Sargasso Sea for another two weeks. Every time the men saw a sea bird or any other living thing, be it seaweed or whale, it was to them a sign of land. Towards the end of the month, the log records seeing and catching dorado – a remarkable and tasty fish that lives in tropical blue waters – and about the same time spotted a tropical wanderer, the frigate bird.

This bird is a pirate of the high seas. It harries other more adept fish-catchers, such as boobies and tropic birds, until they throw up their hard-won catch, which the frigate bird then catches before the fish falls to the sea's surface. Frigate birds are also ace sky-fishers, able to swoop down and pluck flying fish from the air as they glide over the surface of the sea. The dorados and the frigate birds had already made Columbus's acquaintance in the tropical waters off Africa, adding to the expectancy of land. In their anxiety, the crew began to make false sightings which made the situation worse. On Sunday, 7 October 1492, Columbus's fleet of three ships, the *Santa Maria*, the *Pinta* and the *Nina*, had been at sea for 30 days.

PREVIOUS PAGES: A charming if fanciful depiction of early sailors encountering flying fish. Columbus witnessed many such wonders of the open ocean on his first voyage.

Since in the afternoon they had not seen land that the men of the Caravel Nina *thought they had seen; and because great multitudes of birds were passing from north to south-west, which made it seem likely that they were flying off to sleep on land, or perhaps were fleeing from the winter, which, in the land from which they were coming, must be about to arrive; and because the Admiral knew that most of the islands that the Portuguese hold they discovered through birds, the Admiral agreed to leave the route west and head west-south-west …*

This is an extraordinary moment. Columbus, by sailing in the autumn, had encountered the millions of small songbirds that migrate from North America south to the Caribbean, Central and South America. He had met them over 350 miles from land. However, the sight and sound of the flocks of small birds must have lifted everybody's spirits. Even Columbus, who had so far stubbornly stuck to his planned course, changed his mind and decided to follow the birds in the hope that they would lead him to land. Had he not done this, the voyage would have taken longer, and the increasing unrest among the crew may have led to full-blown mutiny. It may be only a small exaggeration to say that the chance encounter with the autumn migration of warblers saved Columbus and changed the course of world history!

The migration carried on for days, and nights, with the sailors remarking that the flocks of thousands of twittering birds blotted out the moon as they flew overhead. Now Columbus was sailing with the land birds. But once again this 'sure sign' that land was near was to prove illusory. The men grew anxious and restless. The crew of the *Santa Maria*, the flagship, was at the point of mutiny, but on the night of 11 October: 'About 10 o'clock, while standing on the sterncastle, I thought I saw a light … it looked like a little wax candle bobbing up and down'. Whether the light was wishful imagining or not, later that night an island was sighted by men aboard the *Pinta*. The small ships had traversed the Atlantic Ocean. The sailors were relieved, Columbus thought he had arrived in Asia, and the world was about to change for ever.

Most scholars of Columbus agree that his first landfall was in the Bahamas, but they disagree about which of the multitude of small islands or cays (a Taino word) he came ashore upon on the morning of 12 October, 1492. Columbus noted: ' … soon we saw naked people'. These were the Lucayo Taino. They called their island Guanahaní, Columbus renamed it San Salvador, Holy Saviour. In front of a crowd of naked Lucayo, he unfurled the flags, erected a cross, and ordered his captains and men: 'to bear witness that I was taking possession of this island for the King and Queen'. It was not an era when one bothered to inquire of the incumbent owners their opinions of the ceremony. The Lucayo Taino were

Dorado, a bizarre-looking, but good tasting, fish of blue water. Its colour changes to reflect its emotional state.

outside the 'civilizing' influence of the Holy Church. Columbus, with the backing of the Pope and Spanish court, felt no compunction in claiming the land and making the heathen 'Indians' Spanish subjects.

It was Columbus himself who first used the term 'Indios' to describe the locals whom he erroneously believed to be the people of the East. In his log, he wrote: 'They were all very well formed, with handsome bodies and good faces. Their hair [is] coarse, almost like the tail of a horse – and short. They wear their hair down over their eyebrows except for a little in back which they keep long and never cut.'

Columbus traded with the Lucayo, who appeared to him not only to have no clothes but no weapons either:

I, in order that they would be friendly to us – because I recognised that they were people who would be better … converted to our Holy Faith by love than by force – to some of them I gave red caps, and glass beads which they put on their chests, and many other things of small value, in which they took so much pleasure and became so much our friends that it was a marvel. Later they came swimming to the ships' launches where we were and brought us parrots and cotton thread in balls …

Columbus noted that the Taino painted their bodies, some with red and white and some with black.

Columbus's 'trade items' must have fascinated the Taino, who had no glass, no metal technology and no concept of money. He noted that one overeager Taino grasped the blade of a sword with his hands and cut himself!

Glass beads, along with brass buckles, coins and some pottery, have been uncovered by archaeologists on modern San Salvador. (Modern San Salvador is a Bahamian cay, formerly called Watlings Island. It was renamed in 1926 by the colonial government which believed it was Columbus's San Salvador. It might have been, but then again it might not. Confusing.)

In his observations of the Lucayo 'Indians', Columbus was quick to note that they wore gold.

I have been very attentive to them, and have tried very hard to find out if there is any gold here. I have seen a few natives who wear a little piece of gold hanging from a hole made in the nose. By signs, if I interpret them correctly, I have learned that by going to the south, I can find a king who possesses a lot of gold and has large containers of it.

On 14 October, Columbus sailed with six Taino guides. He wanted to find the mainland of Asia, and needed to find gold. He recognized that Europe could only fund its expansion and trade deficit with the rest of the world with gold as payment. The gold and riches of the Orient awaited. First, Columbus had to navigate through the myriad islands that he believed lay between him and his objective, Cipango and the coast of Asia. The Tainos of San Salvador told him that the people on the next island had gold. Columbus was suspicious that the natives just wished to escape as soon as possible. Sure enough, two of the guides slipped away in the couple of hours Columbus spent on the island. As Columbus feared, there was no gold.

On his meandering path, guided by Tainos with whom he shared not one word of language, Columbus gives us our first descriptions of the nature of the 'New World'. The next island had more Indians, 'naked as their mothers bore them', and was covered in plants very different from those in Europe. 'All of the trees are as different from ours as day is from night … and so are the fruits, the herbage, the rocks, and everything.' Columbus may have been a great navigator and observer of sea currents and winds, but he was no biologist. What he lacked

The fateful encounter. Columbus makes landfall in the New World, and claims the lands and the people for the king and queen of Spain.

in training he made up for in the enthusiasm of his portrayals. He describes wondrous trees,

very different from ours, and among them many which had branches of many kinds, and all on one trunk … one branch has leaves like those of a cane, and another like those of a mastic, and thus on a single tree [there are] five or six of these kinds, and all very different. Nor are they grafted … Rather, these trees are wild …

What Columbus was almost certainly looking at, or remembering, was a bromeliad, or air plant, attached to the branches of a tree! As we have seen from earlier chapters, the humid climate of the Caribbean has created lush vegetation that everywhere is bedecked in bromeliads.

Columbus wrote ecstatically about the fish of the tropical seas. His diary reads like a postcard from a modern tourist still wet from snorkelling over a Caribbean reef.

Here the fish are so different from ours that it is a marvel. There are some shaped like dories, of the finest colours in the world: blues, yellows, reds, and of all the colours; and others coloured in a thousand ways. And all the colours are so fine that there is no man who would not marvel and take great delight in seeing them.

At the next island, where Columbus waited for more mythical gold, he wrote further nature notes:

And when I arrived here at this cape the smell of the flowers or trees that came from the land was so good and soft that it was the sweetest thing in the world … The flocks of parrots that darken the sun and the large and small birds of so many species are so different from our own that it is a wonder.

Although a great deal has changed in 500 years since Columbus sailed through, those parrots are still in the Bahamas. They are ably studied and protected by dedicated scientists (see next chapter).

Columbus sailed to an island his guides called Colba. It became Cuba in Columbus's log, and has stayed as that ever since – one of the world's great 'typos'! The Taino on Cuba reinforced Columbus's opinion of these people as gentle and, 'very timid, naked, as has been said before, without weapons and without law. These lands are very fertile; the Indians have them full of *mames* [manioc] which are like carrots and have the taste of chestnuts … '

The admiral still thought that Cuba was Japan, and there he sought the gold that he knew was to be found in the Orient. Once again the Taino guides encouraged him in his beliefs. Columbus sent men inland to look for gold, and they reported a strange local habit: 'On the way inland, my two men found many people who were going to different villages, men and women, carrying firebrands in their hands and herbs to smoke, which they are in a habit of doing'. Columbus had stumbled across tobacco, and his log entry is the first European record. But, of course, there was no gold. Instead they came across the strange Taino barkless dogs, kept as food, and more manioc and beans.

Columbus sailed east to an island the Taino guides called Bohio. Here, yet again, gold was promised. Columbus named this large island La Isla Espaniola, 'Spanish Island', which has changed over time to Hispaniola. Once again, the admiral noted that the people were gentle:

> *They do not have arms and they are all naked, and of no skill in arms, and so very cowardly that a thousand would not stand against three. And so they are fit to be ordered about and made to work, plant, and do everything else that might be needed …*

This time Columbus found gold in the form of the *guanin*, ornaments worn by the local Taino chief or *cacique*, Guacanagarí. Columbus lost his flagship, the *Santa Maria*, on Christmas Eve. Undeterred he unloaded the boat with the help of the cacique.

Naked native Americans. One is shown partaking of the curious pastime of smoking.

Yesterday [Christmas Day] Guacanagarí gave us as many canoes as we needed and the labour to unload the ship, and not even a breadcrumb was taken. They are so loyal and respectful of the property of others, and this King is even more honest than the others.

The admiral built a fort, Villa de la Navidad (Christmas Town!) from the timbers of the wreck, and leaving about 40 of his men there, he sailed on eastwards.

At Samana Bay, Columbus had one more encounter with Tainos or Caribs. These people appeared different to Columbus. They were the first people he had seen with bows and arrows, their hair was long and kept in a net of parrot feathers, and they were 'ugly and their faces were stained with charcoal'. Initially arrows were fired, but after the tense start 'a crown of gold' was exchanged for trinkets. Were these the warlike Island-Caribs of the Lesser Antilles on a raiding party?

On 16 January 1493, Columbus set sail for Spain with his Taino guides, some gold and his accounts of the fabulous rich lands of the east. He arrived a hero. The Spanish court marvelled at the Taino Indians (what did *they* make of the court of Ferdinand and Isabella?), the bright parrots, the gold artefacts, and most of all the stories of the riches that the new discoveries promised.

PREVIOUS PAGES: The island of San Salvador in the Bahamas is considered by many scholars to be Columbus's first landfall.

BELOW: The most common means of gold extraction on Hispaniola was panning and sifting the gravel of stream beds.

Spanish colonies in the Caribbean

Columbus returned to the 'West Indies' in the autumn of 1493. The first voyage had been speculative, an exploration. This time he had a fleet of 17 ships, a multitude of men (but strangely no women) and all the paraphernalia for the establishment of a colony on Hispaniola. Ramón Pané, the priest, who would write the only account of the Taino religion, sailed on this voyage. Columbus was ordered by the king and queen to build gold mines, develop trade with the Taino and to convert them to Christianity.

The admiral arrived back at La Navidad on 28 November to find the fort destroyed and all the men he had left behind the previous year dead. The dream of piles of gold died then, and with it any hope of a peaceful colonization. The local *cacique*, Guacanagarí, told Columbus that the Spaniards had mistreated the Taino, taking their women as concubines and stealing their gold. Caonabo, a *cacique* from southern Hispaniola, had retaliated, killing the undisciplined greedy adventurers and destroying La Navidad. Columbus, as ever, was undeterred. He built the first colonial town and named it La Isabela, after the Spanish queen. The town was located on the coast near the gold-field that had been discovered on his first voyage. Columbus's commercial intentions were clear: mercury and Spanish-made crucibles, both needed for gold-mining, have been excavated from this first settlement. The goldrush had begun. Columbus went on to explore Cuba and Jamaica, his quest as much for gold as for the mainland of Asia. He was disappointed on both counts.

The colony of Isabela was not proving a success. The gold-fields were not producing enough gold. The colony moved to the south coast and a new town of Santo Domingo was established. Columbus's venture was facing serious problems. The men he brought on the first voyage were not disciplined sailors but adventurers. Their mistreatment of the Taino set the tone for the colonization of the Americas. During Columbus's protracted absence from Hispaniola, while on his second voyage, the colonists stole the Taino's goods and raped their women. The goodwill that had greeted Columbus on his first voyage was gone for ever. Some of the Taino fled to the hills to avoid the colonists, others were brought into slavery.

Columbus instigated a regime of forced labour. The Taino, at least all those over the age of 14, were to deliver a hawk's bell (the bell attached to a falconer's bird) filled with gold every three months, and if they failed in this imposition the penalty was death. The demand was as unrealistic as it was harsh. The Taino were forced to neglect their fields to pan for gold, so that they couldn't adequately feed themselves, let alone the Spanish colonists who expected to live off their labours. There were periodic uprisings but, with no weapons to compare with those of the colonists, the Taino were doomed and the population began to decline.

The Spaniards, too, had their problems. The colonists were fighting among themselves. In 1500, Columbus was sent back to Spain in disgrace, leaving only 300 Spaniards of the original 1200 settlers. He was an excellent sailor, but a poor administrator. From a Taino perspective, however, his replacements were far worse. The Native Americans were being overworked in the gold-mines and on the ranches. With no time for them to hunt or grow their own crops, malnutrition and famine swept the land that Columbus had described as flowing with milk and honey. They were tortured and slaughtered, so much so that many ran away or committed suicide rather than face life under Spanish rule. By 1509 the 'Indian' population that had numbered as many as a million had been reduced to 60 000 – all working for the Spaniards as virtual slaves.

The following words, those of a Dominican priest, and later Bishop, Bartolomé de Las Casas, who arrived at Santo Domingo, in what is now Haiti in 1502, are surely one of the most gruesome and telling passages in any historic document:

… the island of Hispaniola was the first to witness the arrival of Europeans and the first to suffer the wholesale slaughter of its people and the devastation and depopulation of the land. It all began with the Europeans taking native women and children both as servants and to satisfy their own base appetites …

They forced their way into native settlements, slaughtering everyone they found there, including small children, old men, pregnant women, and even women who had just given birth. They hacked them to pieces, slicing open their bellies with their swords as though they were so many sheep herded into a pen. They even laid wagers on whether they could manage to slice a man in two at a stroke, or cut an individual's head from his body, or disembowel him with a single blow of their axes. They grabbed suckling infants by the feet and, ripping them from their mother's breasts, dashed them headlong against the rocks. Others laughing and joking all the while, threw them over their shoulders into a river, shouting: 'Wriggle, you little perisher.' They slaughtered anyone and everyone in their path, on occasion running through a mother and her baby with a single thrust of their swords. They spared no one,

erecting especially wide gibbets on which they could string their victims up with
their feet just off the ground and then burn them alive thirteen at a time, in honour
of our saviour and the twelve Apostles …

By the first decade of the sixteenth century, the Spanish colonists were
beginning to adapt to the tropics – there were about 10 000 in 15 towns on
Hispaniola. In 1508, they set up a colony on Borinquen, which they named
Puerto Rico. The settlements were motivated by, and built beside, the gold-fields.

Jamaica was the next island to fall. There was no gold here, but the Spanish
needed food and labour for their new colonies in Central and South America. In
1509, Juan de Esquivel conquered the island and its inhabitants, thought to
number 100 000. By 1515, when his term as governor of the island ended, there
were very few Indians left. Las Casas, writing about the islands of Jamaica and
Puerto Rico, said:

Here they perpetrated the same outrages and committed the same crimes as before,
devising yet further refinements of cruelty, murdering the native people, burning and
roasting them alive, throwing them to wild dogs and then oppressing, tormenting and
plaguing them with toil down the mines and elsewhere, so once again killing off these
poor innocents to such effect that where the native population of the two islands was
certainly over six hundred thousand (and I personally reckon it at more than a
million) fewer than two hundred survive on each of the two islands.

The terrible decline of the Taino population led to a labour crisis for the
mines. In just four years from 1509 the whole population of the Bahamian
archipelago, over 40 000 people, were shipped out as slaves. The islands where
Columbus had come ashore were totally deserted. So rapid was the departure and
demise of the Lucayo Taino that Columbus's *diario* of October 1492 is the only
eyewitness account of these people.

Cuba was invaded in 1511. Las Casas, still an adventurer at this point,
travelled with Pánfilo de Narváez. While not a witness to all the events he wrote
about so graphically, much of his description is based on personal experience. He
records the response of Hatuéy, a Taino *cacique*, who had fled with his people from
Hispaniola to escape the cruelty of the Spaniards:

When he heard that the Christians had now switched their attention to Cuba, he
gathered most if not all his people about him and addressed them, saying: 'You know
that the rumour has it that the Christians are coming to this island, and you already
know what they have done to the lord so-and-so and so-and-so and so-and-so. What

they did on Haiti [which is another name for Hispaniola] they will do again here.
Does any of you know why it is that they behave in this way?' And when they
answered him: 'No, unless it be that they are innately cruel and evil', he replied: 'It
is not simply that. They have a God whom they worship and adore, and it is in
order to get that God from us so that they can worship Him that they conquer us
and kill us.' He had beside him, as he spoke, a basket filled with gold jewellery and
he said: 'Here is the God of the Christians.'

Las Casas continues his tale, describing the capture of Hatuéy and his burning at the stake. Before he was set alight, a Franciscan friar informed him of the Christian life hereafter and of the nature of heaven and hell. Hatuéy's response is as acute and acid as his comments on the Christian god of gold:

The lord Hatuey thought for a short while and then asked the friar whether Christians
went to Heaven. When the reply came that the good ones do, he retorted, without need
for further reflection, that, if that was the case, then he chose to go to Hell to ensure he
would never again have to clap eyes on those cruel brutes.

Las Casas saw more atrocities on Cuba:

On one occasion, when the locals had come some ten leagues out from a large
settlement in order to receive us and regale us with victuals and other gifts, and had
given us loaves and fishes and any other foodstuffs they could provide, the Christians
were suddenly inspired by the Devil and, without the slightest provocation,
butchered, before my eyes, some three thousand souls – men, women and children –
as they sat there in front of us.

The *encomienda*

What was the Spanish perception of the events in their new colonies? The Catholic monarchs, Ferdinand and Isabella, who had commissioned Columbus's voyages, were concerned that the colonies be governed in a just and Christian fashion. They later forbade Columbus to ship slaves back to Europe for profit. However the distance between the Castilian court and the new frontiers in the Americas was huge, travel slow and communication unreliable at best. The monarchs were also worried that the settlers might carve up the new land between themselves. The king and queen were right to be anxious. How could they keep control of their new lands? The granting of land to any one settler could cause jealousies and unrest. This might lead to fighting, and, worse, loss of power and revenue that rightly belonged to the Castilian crown.

The monarchs' solution was to hold on to all land. No colonist could own any part of the New World; in compensation, the colonists were to manage the land and the native people on it. The native 'Indians' would be offered the protection of the crown and be given instruction in the Catholic faith in return for their labours. They were also supposed to receive a small wage. This system of *encomienda* – the Indians being 'assigned' to an *encomendero*, to whom they 'were entrusted' – was the foundation of the Spanish colonization. What really happened was that the Taino became slaves. Las Casas himself was an *encomendero*, both on Hispaniola and Cuba, before he gave up the 'stewardship' of his Indians in 1514. Las Casas spent the rest of his life trying to overturn the system which he came to understand as a 'mortal pestilence'.

The shock of the meeting of two totally different cultures took its toll. The native people continued their inevitable decline. The cruelty, hard labour, poor conditions and lack of food, all contributed to the demise of whole populations. Some Indians, so dispirited by their life under the Spanish, committed suicide, using the poisonous juice of bitter cassava. Women abandoned their babies, others refused to bear children. What was there to live for? In 1514, there were only 22 726 Taino on Hispaniola registered as able to work on the *encomiendas*. By 1517 the number had fallen to 11 000. The gold-mines did not survive long. The original gold-fields on Hispaniola were worked out by the 1520s, and those on Puerto Rico and Cuba were exhausted in the next ten years. Now the *encomiendas* were devoted to ranching and sugar cane.

Sugar plantations

Sugar, which quickly overtook gold as the backbone economy of the Caribbean islands, was first planted at La Isabela in 1493, but large-scale plantations did not begin in earnest until well into the next century. By 1545, there were 29 sugar mills recorded on Hispaniola. Sugar cane grows on relatively flat land, and so insatiable was the European sweet tooth that soon most of the suitable low-lying land had been cleared of its luxuriant forests and transformed into prairies of four-metre high grass. As the forests retreated, so did the birds, frogs and reptiles. The sugar plantations were one of the first European influences on the wildlife of the New World. To run them, the Spanish colonists needed labour and lots of it.

Slaves, already put to work in the sugar-cane fields of the Canary Isles, may have arrived in Hispaniola as early as 1509. The first big shipment of African slaves was in 1511. By 1524 there were more slaves than Taino, and, by 1540, the colonists had killed off the native workforce and the Taino had vanished from the census records. The colonists were certainly not going to sweat and toil themselves, so a new source of labour was needed. Black slaves were already at

work, on a small scale, in Europe. They had been shipped by the Portuguese from Africa. Now the shipment of shackled humans grew to grotesque proportions. The Caribbean was the birthplace of large-scale slavery and the African slaves were even worse off than the Taino before them. There was no pretence that they were being 'cared for', helped and educated into the Catholic Church, that a small wage was due, or that they had any choice in the matter. They were there as labourers, considered racially inferior to their owners, and they and their children's lot was permanent slavery.

The plantation slavery, established in the Caribbean colonies, spread throughout the Americas as Europeans, British, Dutch, French and Portuguese, as well as the Spanish, annexed and partitioned the New World. Some ten million Africans are estimated to have been captured, enslaved and transported to the Americas in the 200 years from 1600, most of them to work on sugar plantations. In the next century, African slaves would work the cotton and tobacco fields of the USA. Eventually the Civil War abolished a life of servitude for four-and-a-half million blacks in the southern states.

The attitudes to fellow humans and the land that emerged in the Caribbean spread with the new colonists and helped shape the subjugation of the continents of North and South America. In the Caribbean the importation of slaves changed the ethnic make-up of the region. Today, the nations of the Caribbean have a substantial black population, and, in some countries such as Haiti and Jamaica, the descendants of African slaves are in the majority. The present make-up of the people of the Caribbean is due to the plantations.

The work on the sugar-cane plantations was even more gruelling than the gold-mines. Two crops a year were grown and harvested. The conditions in the fields and the refineries were terrible. Physical abuse was added to long days of gruelling labour, and high humidity and temperatures. One of the reasons the Africans survived the stress of their horrific conditions was because they were less susceptible to the European diseases than the Tainos. Africa and Europe had long shared their microbes and pestilences.

Biological warfare

The native people had been separated from the rest of the world for 13 000 years, ever since they had crossed the low-lying marshes of Beringia, the land bridge that connected Asia to Alaska at the end of the last Ice Age. When the world warmed and the sea levels rose, the Americans were isolated genetically as well as geographically. They had diseases, but they were not the same as those of Europe. As a result, the native people had no resistance, no 'immunity' built up over generations, or within an individual lifetime, to European diseases.

When the Spaniards arrived they brought the germs of biological warfare hidden within them: smallpox, measles, diphtheria, typhoid fever, cholera and scarlet fever were all new and lethal. Even influenza, the common flu, was a killer. At this time, these diseases still killed people in Europe, but mainly the weaker members of society: the very young and old. Most healthy adults, who survived childhood attacks, had a level of resistance to disease. European society functioned because there were plenty of adults to run governments, farm the land, man the

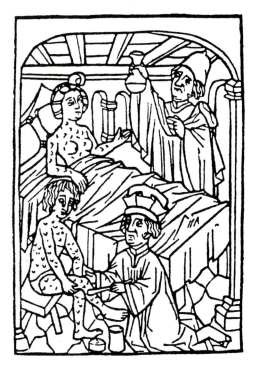

warships or fill the armies. In contrast, Native American societies were felled by European diseases. All ages were affected, all ages died, and the disease swept through communities at the same time, leaving no adults to grow crops, prepare food or even bury the many dead. The diseases were cataclysmic and, combined with the already-mentioned cruelty and malnutrition, they brought about the demise of the Taino in the Caribbean.

Syphilis wreaks havoc in Europe. In less than five years from Columbus's first voyage the disease had broken out in much of Europe, and within the space of a decade it had reached India and China.

Disease, then, played a large part in the conquest of the New World. When Pizarro conquered Cuzco, the Inca capital, in 1533, he had invisible help – smallpox had already arrived. In an earlier conquest, disease played an even bigger role. The Aztec Empire in the early sixteenth century spread in influence from present-day El Salvador to the border of the USA. The capital, Tenochtitlán, was a city of over 200 000 people. The Aztecs were a fierce warlike people who controlled trade over a vast empire of millions of people. Their army, led by jaguar and eagle knights, was feared throughout Central America. Yet this civilization, the greatest military power in the Americas, collapsed in the face of Hernán Cortés and his army of a few hundred Spanish conquistadors. Why? Smallpox. After a siege of 93 days Cortés entered Tenochtitlán, the Aztec capital that sat on an island in the middle of a lake. His triumph was soured by a terrible discovery, described by Bernal Díaz in *The Conquest of New Spain*.

> *We could not walk without treading on the bodies and heads of dead Indians. I have read about the destruction of Jerusalem, but I do not think the mortality was greater there than here in Mexico, where most of the warriors who had crowded in from all the provinces and subject towns had died. As I have said, the dry land and the stockades were piled with corpses. Indeed, the stench was so bad that no one could endure it … even Cortés was ill from the odours which assailed his nostrils.*

How many actually died of European diseases is very difficult to calculate, but some suggest that the population of Mexico would have been approximately 11 million in 1519. Twenty-one years later, it was under six-and-a-half million, and by the end of the century was only two-and-a-half million. The psychological impact of the diseases must have been as devastating as the physical. Here were illnesses and symptoms never before experienced, with no traditional wisdom to explain their occurrence. They killed only the Indians, not the invading Spaniards. What were the few surviving Native Americans to think? The gods of the conquistadors must be protecting them, or at least be more powerful than their gods. The way to avoid disease and death was to become a Christian. The people gave up their old gods and joined the Catholic Church in droves. The conquest of Latin America was religious as well as political.

A curious fact, noted earlier in this chapter, was that the Spanish colonists of 1493 arrived without any women – a strange way to start a permanent occupation. The result, of course, was that the Spaniards and Tainos had sexual contact. This spread diseases, mostly from the Spanish men to the local women, but there were some exceptions: new diseases, such as polio, encephalitis, hepatitis and, in particular, syphilis, spread from the Tainos to the Spaniards. In the words of Las Casas, the scribe:

I repeatedly questioned the natives who confirmed that the disease was endemic in Hispaniola. And there is plenty of evidence that any Spaniard who was unchaste while there caught the infection: indeed scarcely one in a hundred escaped its terrible and continual torments.

There is evidence that, before Columbus's voyages, syphilis was unknown in Europe. Other scientists believe that there was syphilis in Europe, but a new, very virulent strain came back from the colonies. It is quite possible that sailors on the first voyage brought the disease to Europe. Wherever it broke out, syphilis was dreaded. The disease replaced the Black Death as the terror of humankind.

The bark of the *Lignum vitae* tree, a native of the Bahamas, was imported as a cure or, at least, a palliative. It is rumoured that, by the seventeenth century in the markets of Europe, the bark was more costly, by the ounce, than gold. *Lignum vitae*, the wood of life, is the national tree of Jamaica. It is a pretty tree with a blush of blue blossoms. The irony is that the tree is not native to Jamaica. It was introduced in the eighteenth century to provide a cure for the rampant syphilis in the British Army barracks.

The Columbian Exchange

The Columbian Exchange is, in a way, the sum of over 500 years of European and American interaction, and we have already examined some of it. Gold was taken from America to Europe to pay for that continent's expansion of trade. The

The native people of Central America had no beasts of burden. Here, Aztecs are shown carrying Cortés's weapons. He and his men, of course, rode on horseback.

exchange of diseases brought smallpox and death to millions of Native Americans. The obverse was the arrival of syphilis in Europe and, with it, new sexual mores. Some exchanges were all one-way. Africans were brought as slaves to the New World and that terrible trade, in conjunction with the effect of European diseases, has created the mix of races and genes that today is the people of the Americas.

Some of the most profound consequences of the Columbian Exchange were brought about by the most commonplace creatures: horses.

The first horses in the New World arrived at Hispaniola in 1493, as part of Columbus's colonization fleet. That is not strictly true, for horses evolved in North America, at least the best fossil evidence of equines comes from that continent. But horses had been absent from the continent for thousands of years. As ranching overtook gold-extraction in the economy, horses took on a more important role. The New World shrank under the hooves of the Spanish horses. Ranches could grow in size and, inevitably, the native forest retreated in front of the new horse-borne European landowners.

When horses were taken from Cuba to mainland Mexico by Hernán Cortés in 1519, they changed history. The two-year journey from the coast to Tenochtitlán was made easier by horses. The horses not only carried the Spaniards and their loads in a literal sense, they also carried them head and shoulders above the local people who were awe-struck by the giant animals. The horse gave Cortés a huge psychological advantage in his campaign. Montezuma, the Aztec emperor, even had a prophecy that men would arrive on antlerless deer.

From Mexico, the horse escaped on to the huge grasslands that composed much of North America. In the mid-seventeenth century a curious twist of fate took place. The Indians acquired the horse. A century later, the horse was in the hands of the native peoples of the prairies. It was the most perfect match: the horse, the vast prairies and the nomadic lifestyle of the native peoples, the Blackfoot and the Sioux, who became the most expert horsemen. The horse provided transport, and shrank the sea of grass. It allowed a new, safer and more effective means of hunting buffalo, and, very importantly, became a weapon of war.

When the white settlers moved west across the prairies they met native people who had lived with the horse for decades. The Plains Indians, mounted on the descendants of Spanish horses, fought off European-American settlers. The horse-borne US Army finally beat the native cavalry and it was the beginning of the end for the Plains Indians. The horizons that had expanded across the vast grassland with the arrival of the horse now shrank to the boundaries of a reservation.

Many of the new wave of settlers were farmers and ranchers. The horse, combined with cattle, would change the face of the Americas.

Cattle and farmyard animals

The arrival of cattle spelt doom for much of the vegetation of the New World. There were the huge populations of feral cattle on the pampas of Argentina from the sixteenth century. On the plains of the USA, the steer supplanted the buffalo. Once, there had been endless plains covered in a hundred million buffalo, now there were ranches, fences, millions of cattle and just a few remnant herds of bison. The cattle and other farm animals arrived on the second voyage. On Hispaniola they appear to have had free range. The cattle grew to a huge size and were, by all contemporary accounts, fearsome beasts. Pigs had even greater freedom than the cattle. The Caribbean suited them admirably. They went feral, and there are still populations of wild pigs on several Caribbean islands. The fate of the Jamaican iguana was almost sealed by the wild 'porkers'.

The Spanish colonists were quick to benefit from the pigs' success in adapting to the New World and novel climate, and they released pigs on to many islands. To the detriment of native plants, ground-nesting birds and terrestrial lizards, the pigs settled in and multiplied. Where native life lost out, the Spaniards benefited. They had the sport of the hunt and fresh meat whenever they visited the islands. Cattle-ranching has led to the clearance of much tropical forest in Central America and the Caribbean, and has been one of the greatest destroyers of tropical habitat this century.

Columbus encountered fields of maize on his first voyage when he was in Cuba. The word maize comes from a Taino word *maiz*, although the native Caribbean people depended more on cassava or *yuca*. But for most of Central America, maize was the staple of life. Maize kernels almost certainly came to Europe on Columbus's return in 1493, but were never widely accepted as a food. The exception was in Italy, where polenta, a thick porridge made from maize, became a staple food. Where maize had a big impact was in Africa. There, it became one of life's staples, along with the native grain of millet and another American import, the root crop cassava. Without maize, today's Africa would be an even poorer and hungrier continent.

Maize came to Africa in two ways. It first travelled south with the Portuguese to their trading ports in West Africa and, from there, spread rapidly into the interior, along the riverine routes of commerce. It is recorded as being grown hundreds of miles up the Niger river as early as 1535. The second migration of maize came directly from the Americas. Slave-traders brought the seeds to pay for their wretched human cargo, which they then shipped to the New World.

The staple food of the native peoples of the Caribbean, cassava was almost certainly brought to the Caribbean by the ancestors of the Taino when they travelled by canoe from South America. It is an undemanding crop that produces more starchy food per hectare than any other. For this reason it is popular in areas with poor soils in Africa and Asia. The pounding of manioc (another name for cassava) is a common sight in villages in the Central African Republic. It is sometimes hard to imagine that this life-supporting root crop has not been in Africa forever. Cassava, like maize, has added to the storehouse of starchy staples, and only millet is more important than these two New World émigrés.

The Taino name *mani* carried straight over to Spanish for this native Caribbean groundnut. Peanuts are still important in the economy of countries, such as The Gambia. Today, more peanuts are grown outside the Americas, with India being the world's largest producer.

Sweet potato was taken to New Guinea by the Portuguese, perhaps as early as the sixteenth century. Traded by the coastal Papuans with their interior neighbours, it caused a revolution when it arrived at the end of the trade routes in the highlands. Up until then, taro (an edible rootstock also called elephant's ear) had been the main crop, but it was not as productive, nor as easy to cultivate as sweet potato. Once the new crop was established, it became a staple of the highland diet and resulted in a population explosion.

Right up until this century the colonial powers had always assumed that the highlands of New Guinea were unpopulated. They sat, remote, above the banks of thick clouds that so often engulfed the coast, and the routes into the interior were hazardous and physically demanding. When the Australians finally penetrated the interior in the 1930s they discovered a huge population, far greater than any they could have dreamed of. There was a richness of cultures, a variety of tribes and languages unmatched anywhere else on the planet. This huge and diverse population, with its 400-year history of wars and allegiances, was due in part to the sweet potato and the Columbian Exchange. New Guinea was the starting point for another revolutionary crop.

Sugar cane is thought to have grown wild in Polynesia, and to have first been domesticated by the people of New Guinea. Somehow, over 2000 years ago, it moved into China. By the Middle Ages, Europe had acquired a taste for sugar. The returning crusaders had experienced its delights in the Near East, and the Moors, who cultivated it in North Africa, introduced it during the conquest of Spain. Sugar cane was cultivated on the Atlantic island of Madeira in the mid-fifteenth century and later on the Canaries. On both outposts of Iberian power, slaves, taken from Africa, were used in the labour-intensive cultivation of this luxury crop. And, as already discussed, history was to repeat itself when Columbus took sugar cane from the Canary Islands with him on his second voyage.

The size of the Spanish sugar plantations on Hispaniola were surpassed by those of the Portuguese in Brazil, and the British in the Caribbean. Many of the

British colonies were transformed by sugar. In the middle of the seventeenth century, the tiny island, Barbados, was nothing but a sea of sticky cane grass, and the largest producer of sugar in the world. The native vegetation, which has never recovered, had been felled by the labour of thousands of black slaves. By the next century, Jamaica had overtaken Barbados as the world's largest exporter, supporting a population of 20 000 white colonists and 200 000 black slaves.

After sugar cane, bananas, originally from Asia, have had the largest impact on the native vegetation of the Caribbean. The economies of many of the Lesser Antilles still depend on the export of them. The lowland slopes of many islands are now a monoculture of banana plants, the 'hands' wrapped in blue clear plastic bags to encourage ripening and keep out bugs.

After Columbus's mention of tobacco in his log for Cuba, this local leaf remained undiscovered by Europeans until the following century. The practice of smoking tobacco seems to have started among the Spanish colonists. Cuba, where Columbus first noted the habit of smoking cigars, still has a thriving tobacco industry. The cigars from Havana are considered to be the finest in the world.

The modern Taino

There is a firmly held view that the Taino became extinct very shortly after the Spanish arrived. The Taino were certainly decimated and much of their culture lost, but were they exterminated? After centuries when native cultures have been denigrated and reviled, new groups are springing up across the Caribbean who are emphasizing their native ancestry. There is a new pride in a heritage that has long been ignored. In Puerto Rico, there are Taino dance and theatre groups that are helping to focus that nation's cultural identity as separate from the USA.

But do the Taino still exist? A great many of the early Spanish colonists married Taino brides, and so Taino blood and Taino culture must have stayed alive within these families. The Spanish census of Hispaniola in 1514, that found so few Taino on the *encomiendas*, revealed that 40 per cent of Spanish men had taken Indian wives. These mixed marriages would have kept some part of the Taino world view alive. While the Taino disappear from the census records in the first part of the sixteenth century, some people hold that they simply were recategorized as peasants, and that these peons of the poor mountainous interior of Puerto Rico, Hispaniola and Cuba, continued to live with Taino traditions and beliefs, often interwoven with Catholicism.

These two sources of knowledge of Taino beliefs and customs may have remained private, kept within the bounds of the families for centuries. With the renewed interest in the unique cultural heritage of the Greater Antilles, a Taino revival has begun.

CHAPTER 11

THE STORY TODAY –
the HORRORS AND
the HOPE

The period since Columbus's arrival has brought great changes to the Caribbean and Central America. There has been wholesale clearance of forests for agriculture, timber and pasture. The forested islands of the Bahamas that Columbus gazed upon in wonder, and romanticized about in his log, have largely gone, to be replaced by scrub and tough grasses. In Costa Rica, Guatemala and Honduras, the natural world has shrunk as ranches, and coffee, banana and citrus fruit plantations have covered ever more of the land. In Mexico, irrigation has turned thousands of hectares of desert into cotton and vegetable farms.

The story is all too familiar, and, from a wildlife point of view, thoroughly depressing. There is no avoiding the reality of the massive loss of habitat or the environmental degradation that has occurred in the last hundred years; nor should we ignore the fact that this process is continuing at this very moment. Central America and the Caribbean are not rich areas. Most of the people struggle to keep their families fed. The ever-increasing population places great pressure on the natural resources. The hunger for land is great. Poverty is not an ally of wilderness conservation.

In many countries the great majority of the land is in the hands of just a few families. Vast cattle-ranches and plantations form a monochromatic mosaic over the landscape. These huge operations have brought great wealth to the few, but at the expense of the wilderness. The wealthiest families control the productivity, the natural riches of the country, and so much of the soil's wealth is directed into cash-crops for export and profit for the few. The poor scrape a living from the margins – from small gardens of maize and beans. Yet despite the horror that is the recent history of the region, there are glimmers of light: isolated events that are harbingers of hope for the future.

Cuba

Cuba is clothed in swathes of swaying sugar cane, its economy dominated by the sweet tooth of Eastern Europeans. Where there is no sugar cane, there are ordered rows of orchards: grapefruits, lemons and oranges. Cuba's highly centralized economy groans under the economic embargo of the USA and the loss of its old Communist trading partners. But, despite its problems, there are people inside the government who are dedicated to preserving Cuba's wildlife and wilderness.

Dr Roberto Soberón is a shy quietly-spoken man. A chief scientist with Empresa Nacional de Preservación de Flora y Fauna, he is a highly educated, caring person with a mission to help his country and the endangered, rascally Cuban crocodile.

PREVIOUS PAGES: The lush richness of undisturbed tropical forest, as seen from the air.

In the Lanier swamp on the Isla de Juventud, the government has set up a crocodile farm. Crocodiles were transported from their last stronghold, the vast Zapata swamp on the south coast of the main island. In their new swamp, in large naturally planted enclosures, Cuban crocs are successfully breeding. The adult males and females, robust, heavily-armoured beasts, three to four metres in length, mate in the months of April and May. The courtship is a gentle affair, with both behemoths cruising slowly, side by side, through the water. When the prolonged preliminary foreplay is complete and the female is ready to accept the male, she sinks below the water and turns over. The male swims to her. They mate, belly to belly, without any great drama, the male atop the female, and both beasts almost vertical in the water. He keeps his head above the water, and the completely submerged female's head breaks the surface for the occasional breath. To a naive observer, the whole affair comes as a surprise. There is no violence, no great thrashings, no foaming water, just silent swirls of dark water as the fiercest of beasts conduct the gentlest of lovemaking. The performance is balletic, or, perhaps more accurately, the world's finest example of synchronized swimming.

The outcome of the efforts of Dr Soberón, his colleagues and crocodile wards, is a highly successful breeding programme. All around the breeding enclosure there are large well-planted pens full of feisty adolescent crocodiles. These well-fed beasts have all the aggression of their cousins in the wild. A walk alongside their pen is accompanied by the constant crashing of crocodile bodies against the mesh fence. The experience is a little disconcerting as, one after another, crocodiles hurtle through the air at head-height on their collision-course trajectory. Only the thin woven wire, less than a metre away, arrests the crocodiles' intent.

There is a second crocodile farm beside the Zapata swamp, and the result of their joint efforts is a hopeful future for the crocodiles. The purpose of the farms is not purely preservation. The farms produce meat and hides. They are a practical mix of conservation and commerce. In today's world, if an animal can prove its financial worth, then it stands a far greater chance of survival. There is no doubting Dr Soberón's passion for or commitment to the survival of crocodile. With his endeavours, and those of the Cuban government, the Cuban crocodile is safe at present and may eventually return to some of its ancient haunts.

Jamaica

The most splendid of all the West Indian butterflies lives on Jamaica. The *Homerus* swallowtail is huge. The females have a wingspan reaching fifteen centimetres. The largest swallowtail in the New World, this gorgeous giant was first described in 1793. It was originally widespread on the island, living wherever there was plenty of rain, high humidity and its food plant, *Hernanadia*. Today it is confined to just

The Jamaican giant swallowtail. Its size and beauty have been part of its problem.

two sites: the rugged, wooded, limestone Cockpit country to the west and, in the east, the Rio Grande valley that lies between the spectacular John Crow and Blue Mountains. These are still remote areas. To reach them requires a nerve-racking, gut-wrenching, three-hour drive from the capital, Kingston.

The giant swallowtail is in trouble. Its caterpillars need the high humidity of montane rainforests to prosper, but they are being cleared for subsistence-agriculture by the expanding population. The wholesale planting of pines for forestry has removed yet more native forest. Another reason why this butterfly is in trouble is its very beauty. Collectors pay large sums for specimens. In the 1970s and 1980s, the price for a *Homerus* swallowtail ranged from $400 to $1500. And, while 50 years ago, you could hope to see 50 of these impressive insects fluttering and gliding over the forest canopy, today you would be lucky to see one. The butterfly is endangered and declining, beset with problems, but it has friends.

Patti Bedasse is a dynamic conservationist who has set out to inform her fellow Jamaicans about the plight of the swallowtail. Her approach is hard-hitting.

The Cuban Amazon, among the palms it typically uses for nesting.
Only in the Bahamas does this gaudy parrot breed underground.

Huge roadside billboards display the grandeur of the swallowtail, three metres high, and the message is straightforward and strong: take pride in your national wildlife treasures. Along with this eye-catching publicity, Patti has produced informative and entertaining leaflets for schoolchildren, and fun lapel badges. The results are encouraging. The butterfly's plight is now well known, and it will not slip into oblivion unnoticed.

Alongside Patti's work, Dr Eric Garraway has been studying the needs of *Homerus*. His work has shown the butterflies' dependence on the high humidity that is only to be found along streams in the montane rainforest. He has pointed out the dangers of commercial forestry and the planting of Caribbean pine plantations. Dr Garraway combines scientific endeavour with a strong conservation ethic. He is arguing for a national park to protect the last pieces of montane forest, along with their beautiful flyers. There is hope for the butterfly, but the problems have still to be solved.

Bahamas

Ten years ago Rosemarie Gnam gave up a good job to save a parrot from extinction. The bird in question is the Bahamian sub-species of the Cuban Amazon. This parrot, which once lived on all the bigger islands, was the first bird from the New World to arrive in Europe. Columbus returned from his first voyage with some parrots as presents for the king and queen of Spain. Since then, the parrot has faced an increasing number of problems: the felling of native forests, hunting, poaching for the pet trade, and introduction of cats and rats, have all added to its plight. Today the parrots live only on the islands of Abaco and Great Inagua.

What makes the Bahamas parrot unique is its nesting habits. Unlike other members of its tribe, the birds nest underground. The island is composed of coralline limestone and is riddled with holes. The parrots use these holes in preference to cavities in trees. The holes may be two metres deep. Why they nest underground is not known. It might be because the trees on the islands do not offer suitable nest-holes, or it may be that the birds did not need to nest in trees because there were no predators. That is sadly no longer true. Europeans introduced cats and rats to the islands 300 years ago, and cats, in particular, have had a terrible impact.

Dr Gnam's work uncovered the basic biology of the Bahamas parrot, and the threats just mentioned, and, from these, she was able to put forward a plan to save the bird from extinction. In 1992, the quincentenary of Columbus's voyage, the government, the Bahamas National Trust and conservationists, launched a campaign to publicize the parrot. There were posters, car-stickers and even a rap-song.

Today, the parrot still faces the prospect of ending up as cat food, but things are improving. The culling of feral cats is keeping cat numbers down; and the key area of southern Abaco, 6700 hectares of tropical hardwood and pines, is now being managed by the Bahamas National Trust, thus ensuring that the birds will have somewhere to roost and feed.

Haiti

'Haiti is one of the most environmentally degraded countries in the world, and faces serious economic and social problems.' So starts a chapter in *The Biography of the Caribbean* by Professor Charles Woods and associates. Later, he states: 'Haiti is now classified by many as an environmental disaster area'. The sentence is doom-laden, yet Professor Woods has hopes for Haiti, its people and wildlife.

Haiti forms the eastern part of Hispaniola, and, due to the geological collision that created the island, it has a very large number of endemic species. The island is over-populated and its resources over-exploited. The great majority of Haitians are poor subsistence farmers. The increasingly desperate poverty has led to the island being almost completely deforested. With 720 people per hectare of farmed land, and one of the highest population densities in the world, it has only 1.5 per cent forest cover. The population is destined to double in the next 35 years, unless there is some change.

The lush forested mountains are now largely bare and the dry forests are being cleared, even fruit trees have been chopped down for firewood and charcoal. Grinding poverty means the peasants cannot afford to think of tomorrow. The loss of tree cover has led to horrific soil erosion and in many areas the hillsides are beyond repair, the soil has been washed away by fierce rainy-season torrents. Without the trees to hold the moisture, the same streams that flush fertile soil to the sea, dry up for the rest of the year. This, in turn, has created severe problems of water supply. So what is there to be optimistic about?

In 1983, two national parks were created – Pic Macaya and Morne la Visite – both in remote mountainous areas. They protect important areas of forest and, at the same time, ensure that the streams from these areas will flow continuously, and the soil will not wash away. The streams from the two parks supply some of the most important agricultural land in Haiti. The logic of protecting the remaining trees is understood. There is hope, but only if the parks are not degraded by desperate peasants. They must be more than 'paper parks' and that depends on whether the government and international conservation bodies are willing to fund and police parks that will serve both wildlife and the people of Haiti. The answer to that question is not clear. The recent political changes may be the last chance to save Haiti from total ecological Armageddon.

Puerto Rico

The islands of the Greater Antilles were colonized by descendants of the white-fronted Amazon of Central America. They, as we saw in the case of the Bahamas parrot, have fared badly, but none so poorly as the Puerto Rican parrot. It is an extraordinary story. The birds were once common all over the island. Then logging, ranching and agriculture arrived and as the amount of native forest declined from almost a 100 per cent to 0.2 per cent today, the parrot spiralled towards extinction. The decline was dramatic. By the 1930s the parrots could only be found in the Sierra de Luquillo. There were 200 birds in 1937; by 1975 there were 13. Since then, intensive efforts to save the bird have helped push the population back up, but there are major problems. There are still a few breeding pairs in the wild. Predation and parasitism cause some losses, but it is unclear why the wild population does not expand. Perhaps the only remaining wilderness is not the parrots' preferred habitat?

The ravaged face of Haiti. The hard-pressed land has lost its natural forest cover and is now faced with erosion.

The Puerto Rican authorities continue to battle for the birds' survival. Captive breeding has had some success. The aviary population is growing, but the transition to the wild is fraught with dangers. The preservation programme has been long and expensive, and, even with the resources of the US Fish and Wildlife Service, the World Wildlife Fund, and the Puerto Rican Department of Natural Resources, the future of the Puerto Rican parrot is not assured.

Costa Rica

The gorgeously plumed quetzal that bedazzled the Maya has remained an enigma. The Aztec Emperors could not keep it in their menageries, and it is still a mysterious bird. But conservationists are working to discover how to protect this fabulous bird.

In Costa Rica there is only a patchwork of forest left, mostly up on the steep, cloud-covered mountains. This is the home of the quetzal, so, for a long period, conservationists thought the bird was relatively secure. George Powell has been striving to save the quetzal by first discovering the birds' lifestyle. He arrived in Costa Rica in the 1970s, and set about saving the cloud forests that hug the mountain summits of the land bridge. The result is the Monteverde Cloud Forest

Preserve. This privately owned reserve has been bought piecemeal, acre by acre, and largely by citizens from all over the world. It is proof that individuals can make a difference.

The work carried out by George Powell and his Costa Rican colleagues has shown that quetzals need more than their cloud-forest fastness. The scientists attached a tiny six-gram radio transmitter to the birds, then followed them on foot and by light aircraft. The birds migrated down the slopes after breeding. Monteverde was not enough. The forests lower down the slopes would have to be protected if the quetzal was to be saved. The problem is that there is so little forest left, most of the lower slopes have already been converted into cattle pastures. Monteverde itself is a lush green island surrounded by over-grazed grassland.

Powell and his team now know the quetzal's routes down the slopes to the Atlantic and Pacific lowlands. These are narrow forested corridors and, armed with this crucial knowledge, the team now aims to encourage landowners to protect the trees in the quetzal corridors. If they are successful, then the sacred bird of Maya and Aztec may not vanish from yet another of its strongholds. The signs are good.

Paseo Pantera

This is the most ambitious conservation project of all. Paseo Pantera is the plan to co-ordinate the efforts of organizations and governments throughout Central America, and create a green corridor of habitat along the length of the land bridge. The plan is bold and holds the greatest hope for the region. The seven countries of the land bridge would maintain and create parks and reserves to protect both the traditional way of life of native people and the biodiversity of the area. The parks are designed to link by way of buffer zones, thus, for the first time, giving larger mammals a chance to spread and migrants suitable habitat on their long journeys. This co-ordinated multinational approach may help protect the many native cultures, including the Maya, as well as save the multitude of species of plants and animals that make this region the most fascinating on earth.

The Caribbean and Central America has been 150 million years in the making. During that long period, plants and animals have found ways of arriving and adapting to this new land. In turn, the land and its wildlife have helped shape some of the most remarkable cultures on earth. The Taino, Aztec and Maya civilizations have disappeared. The wildlife, such as jaguars and quetzals, has every chance of surviving, but only if we care.

Further Reading

Natural History

Colbert, Edwin H., *Wandering Lands and Animals*, Hutchinson 1974

Forshaw, Joseph M. and Cooper, William T., *Parrots of the World*, Lansdowne Editions 1989

Stokes, W. Lee, *Essentials of Earth History*, Prentice-Hall 1982

Tyrell, Esther and Robert, *Hummingbirds of the Caribbean*, Crown Publishers 1990

Woods, Charles A. (ed.), *Biogeography of the West Indies, Past, Present and Future*, Sandhill Crane Press 1989

The Civilizations

Coe, Michael D., *Mexico, from the Olmecs to the Aztecs*, Thames & Hudson, 4th Edition 1994

Kerchache, Jacques, *L'Art Taino*, Musées de la Ville de Paris 1994

Miller, Mary and Taube, Karl, *The Gods and Symbols of Ancient Mexico and the Maya*, Thames & Hudson 1993

Rouse, Irving, *The Tainos, Rise and Decline of the People who Greeted Columbus*, Yale University Press 1992

Stevens-Arroyo, Antonio M., *The Cave of the Jaguar, The Mythical World of the Tainos*, University of New Mexico Press 1988

Taube, Karl, *Aztec and Maya Myths*, British Museum Press 1993

Tedlock, Dennis (tr.), *Popol Vuh, The Mayan Book of the Dawn of Life*, Simon & Schuster 1985

The Post Columbus Period

Casas, Bartolomé de las, *History of the Indies*, Harper Row 1971

Casas, Bartolomé de las, *A Short Account of the Destruction of the Indies*, Penguin Books 1992

Crosby, Alfred W. Jr., *The Columbian Exchange; Biological and Cultural Consequences of 1492*, Greenwood Press 1972

Díaz, Bernal, *The Conquest of New Spain*, Cohen, J.M. (tr.) Penguin Books 1963

Sauer, Carl O., *The Early Spanish Main*, University of California Press 1966

Picture Credits

BBC Worldwide Publishing would like to thank the following for providing photographs and for permission to reproduce copyright material. While every effort has been made to trace and acknowledge all copyright holders, we would like to apologize should there have been any errors or omissions.

AMERICAN MUSEUM OF NATURAL HISTORY p. 205; BBC NATURAL HISTORY UNIT pp. 74 (Hans Christoph Kappel), 75 (Andrew Harrington), 86 & 158-9 *left* (Jürgen Freund), 90 (Gerry Ellis), 98 (Gerry Ellis) & 163 (Doug Weschsler); BRIDGEMAN ART LIBRARY, LONDON p. 139 (British Museum, London); BRITISH LIBRARY p. 192; SARAH BYATT p. 150; BRUCE COLEMAN COLLECTION pp. 2 (M.P.L. Fogden), 26 (Werner Stoy), 30-1 (M.P.L. Fogden), 58 (Joseph van Wormer), 79 (Rod Williams), 95 (John Cancalosi) & 155 (Giorgio Gualco); COMSTOCK p. 171; RUDOLPH DIESEL p. 62 & 63; ELLIS NATURE PHOTOGRAPHY pp. 146-7 (Jeremy Stafford-Deitsch); THOMAS C. EMMEL p. 214; E.T. ARCHIVE pp. 186-7 & 201; M. & P. FOGDEN p. 91; WERNER FORMAN ARCHIVE pp. 102-3 (Private Collection, N.Y.), 118 (Dallas Museum of Fine Art, USA), 142 (Edward H. Merrin Gallery, N.Y.), 174 (National Museum of Anthropology, Mexico City), 178-9, 182 (Museum für Völkerkunde, Basel) & 183; FOTOMAS INDEX pp. 193, 196 & 198; FUNDACION GARCIA AREVALO p. 154; ROBERT HARDING PICTURE LIBRARY pp. 130, 135 *right*, 194-5 & 218; JÜRGEN HOPPE p. 39; DAVID HUGHES pp. 82-3; NEIL LUCAS pp. 67, 166-7 & 215; NHPA pp. 10 (Stephen Dalton), 119 (ANT), 127 (G.I. Bernard) & 210-11 (Martin Wendler); OXFORD SCIENTIFIC FILMS pp. 70-1 (Ken Cole) & 122-3 (M.P.L. Fogden); PLANET EARTH PICTURES pp. 110 (David E. Rowley), 134-5 *left* (Carol Farneti), 159 *right* (Norbert Wu) & 190 (Doug Perrine); G.O. POINAR JNR pp. 50 & 51; MIKE POTTS pp. 22 & 46-7; QUESADA/BURKE STUDIOS, N.Y. p. 111 (Christopher Burke); SCIENCE PHOTO LIBRARY pp. 23 (Tom van Sant/Geosphere Project, Santa Monica), 42 (NASA) & 54 (NASA); ALFONSO SILVA LEE pp. 38, 43 & 59 *top*; SOUTH AMERICAN PICTURES pp. 114-15 (Tony Morrison) & 143 (Chris Sharp); VIREO p. 59 *bottom* (Doug Wechsler); WELLCOME INSTITUTE LIBRARY, LONDON p. 203; ZEFA pp. 6-7 & 18-19; ZOOLOGICAL SOCIETY OF LONDON p. 78.

The drawings on pp. 131 & 137 are from *The Rise and Fall of Maya Civilization* by J. Eric S. Thompson 1954 and are reproduced by courtesy of the University of Oklahoma Press. The woodcuts on p. 165 are from *Isolario* by Benedetto Bordone 1528. The plan on p. 177 is from *Planos de la Cuidad de Mexico*, Mexico City 1938.

Index